CLAWING BACK

CULTURE AND ECONOMIC LIFE

CLAWING BACK

Redistribution in Precarious Times

DEBORAH JAMES

STANFORD UNIVERSITY PRESS
Stanford, California

Stanford University Press
Stanford, California

Library of Congress Cataloging-in-Publication Data
Names: James, Deborah, author.
Title: Clawing back : redistribution in precarious times / Deborah James.
Other titles: Culture and economic life.
Description: Stanford, California : Stanford University Press, 2025. | Series: Culture and economic life | Includes bibliographical references and index.
Identifiers: LCCN 2024042813 (print) | LCCN 2024042814 (ebook) | ISBN 9781503642355 (cloth) | ISBN 9781503642874 (paperback) | ISBN 9781503642881 (ebook)
Subjects: LCSH: Debt—Social aspects—South Africa. | Debt—Social aspects—Great Britain. | Consumer credit—Social aspects—South Africa. | Consumer credit—Social aspects—Great Britain. | Income distribution—South Africa. | Income distribution—Great Britain. | Labor—South Africa. | Labor—Great Britain. | Public welfare—South Africa. | Public welfare—Great Britain.
Classification: LCC HG3756.S6 J35 2025 (print) | LCC HG3756.S6 (ebook) | DDC 332.70968—dc23/eng/20250111
LC record available at https://lccn.loc.gov/2024042813
LC ebook record available at https://lccn.loc.gov/2024042814

Cover design: George Kirkpatrick
Cover photograph: David Neves

To my family, both immediate and extended,
both affines and consanguines

Contents

Illustrations

Acknowledgments

The field research for this book, and the mulling over of its contents, has occurred over a long period, and I have acquired many debts in the process. I am grateful to all who held discussions with me and helped me navigate my way around this difficult topic, as well as to those who furnished funding for it.

For the UK research, there were several tranches of funding, stretching as far back as 2011: first the LSE STICERD grant "Rights Welfare and Law. Legal Aid Advocacy in Austerity Britain," later the LSE Research Committee Seed Fund grant "Rights Welfare and Law. Legal Aid Advocacy in Austerity Britain," and then a Leverhulme Fund grant "Creative Interventions: Innovation in Public Legal Services After Legal Aid." In all these projects I had the good fortune to work collaboratively with Alice Forbess as co-researcher. This investigation culminated in another ESRC grant, "An Ethnography of Advice: Between Market, Society and the Declining Welfare State," which enabled a larger team to conduct research. While the latter grant did not feed directly into this book, I have been informed and inspired while writing it by the many discussions, formal and informal, which I had with the team members—Ryan Davey, Ana Gutiérrez Garza, Tobias Eule, Alice Forbess, Insa Lee Koch, Anna Tuckett, and Matt Wilde—and by their own writings, both published and unpublished, that resulted. All have gone on to do great things, fully justifying the faith I had in their abilities from the beginning of the project. Those wishing to know more are invited to look at the joint publishing effort that came out of the project—a special issue of the journal *Ethnos* on "The State of the Welfare State: Advice, Governance and Care in Settings of Austerity"—as well as the project website https://www.lse.ac.uk/anthropology/people/deborah -james. For help with the research, I am grateful to all those I met who made it possible for Alice Forbess and me to shadow your advice sessions at Citizens Advice, at different Law Centres, at Social Action for Health and its various partner organizations, and in other debt advice offices.

For the South African tranche of the research, I received initial funding from LSE Anthropology's RII Fund, and later the LSE KEI fund—"Welfare Payments as Debt Collateral in South Africa: Collaborating to Challenge Illicit Deductions." With these funds, and under the auspices of Black Sash, I conducted research along with fellow researchers and writers Erin Torkelson and David Neves: thank you for the great experience of teamwork. I owe much to Black Sash, a crucial collaborator in the project overall, and the various members of its partner organizations. Thanks also to Black Sash for a careful reading of this manuscript in advance of publication (opinions and analysis are my own). Subsequent work involved the committed engagement of others in Black Sash: Hoodah Abrahams-Fayker, Rachel Bukasa, Kholiwe Dlali, Gail Kirchner, and Amanda Rinquest, and, at the Credit Ombud, Howard Gabriel and Kabelo Theme. I am indebted to others for their participation: those who assisted me in the field: Clark Gardner, Odette Geldenhuys, Andrew Hutchinson, Odwa Nweba, Stephan van der Merwe, and Sune van der Merwe.

If one measures academic influence and collegiality like ripples spreading out from the center of a pool, the next ring of people to thank are participants in the various workshops that were run as part of these various projects. They include, in particular, Catherine Alexander, Gillian Evans, Lisa Hahn, Toby Kelly, Martijn Koster, Giacomo Loperfido, Richard Moorhead, James Organ, Jennifer Sigafoos, Bev Skeggs, and Katharine Tyler.

I was offered conducive surroundings and valuable insights when I wrote and/or presented versions of the material in this book. My gratitude goes to Andreas Eckert and Fe Hentschke for having me as an invited guest at Re:work, Berlin, and to the fellows who attended and commented on my talk there; to the staff members and co-fellows at the Stellenbosch Institute for Advanced Study, Wallenberg Research Centre, at Stellenbosch University, South Africa, for an encouraging setting while writing up some of the material; to faculty members and colleagues at University of Edinburgh who invited me to give the Munro Lecture; to Kate Meagher and participants in the joint Anthropology of Economy/Inclusive Economies workshop at LSE; to Chris Hann, Don Kalb, Marek Mikuš, and other colleagues at the Max Planck Institute for Social Anthropology in Halle who ran the "Financialisation Beyond Crisis: Connections, Contradictions, Contestations" workshop; Isabelle Guérin and

Hadrien Saiag (sadly no longer with us, and much mourned) who ran the workshop on "Financialization from Below: A Moral and Political Economy of Debt" at Les Plantiers, France; Dinah Rajak, Kate Meagher, and Catherine Dolan who ran the "Infrastructures of Inclusion: Technology, Services, Markets, and Finance" workshop at LSE; Fred Wherry who ran the launch of the "Dignity and Debt Network" at Princeton; Susana Narotzky who ran the "Grassroots Economics: Meaning, Project, and Practice in the Pursuit of Livelihood" conference in Oñati, Spain; Morag McDermont who ran the "Working the Boundaries of Law" workshop in Oñati, Spain; Harry Walker and Mathijs Pelkmans for masterminding the "How People Compare" workshop at LSE; Insa Koch and colleagues at St. Gallen University who invited me to speak at the "Ethnography Talks" series; and Alice von Bieberstein who invited me to IfEE Instituteskolloquium, Humboldt University.

Particularly valuable have been two sets of interactions. One was with the Monday reading group, whose members—Marion Fourcade, Isabelle Guérin, Kaveri Ishwar Haritas, Nicolas Lainez, Jeanne Lazarus, Benjamin-Noel Lemoine, Mariana Luzzi, Marek Mikuš, Fabian Muniesa, Susana Narotzky, Federico Neiburg, Horacio Ortiz, Fareen Parvez, Sarah Quinn, and Ariel Wilkis—have created a warm and stimulating (online) scholarly community. The other was the intense reading and research involved—just before I started writing the book—in a paper co-written with Caitlin Zaloom (with the help of Asprey Liu and Thom Herzmark) for the *Annual Review of Anthropology* (Zaloom & James 2023). Others who offered feedback and support include Karin Barber, Laura Bear, Max Bolt, Becky Bowers, Keith Breckenridge, Joe Deville, Chris Harker, Sam Kirwan, Nikita Simpson, Joe Spooner, Hedwig Waters, and Gisa Weszkalnys. Miranda Sheild Johannson did a detailed reading, and gave valuable advice, as did the two anonymous reviewers. The list goes on, and it would take pages to name everybody—I apologize for any inadvertent omissions. Those not listed here are named in the book.

I owe a particularly substantial debt to the Wissenschaftskolleg zu Berlin—Advanced Study Institute, which hosted me during the sabbatical year during which I wrote the book. Thanks to Barbara Stollberg-Rilinger and Daniel Schonpflug, to all those members of staff who contributed to making our stay there so productive, and to my "fellow-fellows" who offered feedback on my colloquium and generally made the experience so enjoyable.

Finally, for inspiring mentorship in the longer term, I am—as ever—grateful to Adam Kuper. For support and succor, thanks to my children, Ben and Caitlin Pearson, stepchildren Oskar Pearson and Nickle Felgate (and their partners Christina and Nicole), and step-grandchildren Juliet, Ryan and Victor. And for all these (as well as countless chapter readings) I am forever thankful to my husband Patrick Pearson.

Abbreviations

ADRA   Association of Debt Recovery Agents (SA)

ATM   automated teller machine

ATOS   French digital services company, to which the UK government outsourced the assessment of benefits claims (UK)

BIG   basic income grant

CA   Citizens Advice (UK)

CB   child benefit (UK)

CEO   chief executive officer

CFEB   Consumer Financial Education Body (UK)

CLA   Courts of Law Amendment Bill (SA)

CLACS   Community Legal Advice Centres (UK)

CLANS   Community Legal Advice Networks (UK)

COP 27   27th Conference of the Parties of the UNFCCC United National Framework Convention on Climate Change

CPS   Cash Paymaster Services (SA)

CSG   child support grant (SA)

CTC   child tax credit (UK)

DLA   disability living allowance (now replaced by PIP for those between sixteen years and pension age) (UK)

DSD	Department of Social Development (SA)
DTIC	Department of Trade, Industry, and Competition (SA)
DWP	Department of Work and Pensions (UK)
EAO	emoluments attachment order (SA)
EFT	electronic file transfer
EPE	EasyPay Everywhere (SA)
ESA	employment support allowance (UK)
FCA	Financial Conduct Authority (formerly FSA) (UK)
FCG	foster care grant (SA)
FSA	Financial Services Authority (UK)
HB	housing benefit (UK)
HMRC	Her Majesty's Revenue and Customs (UK)
JSA	job seeker's allowance (UK)
LAB	Legal Aid Board (UK)
LDC	less developed countries
LSE	London School of Economics
MaPS	Money and Pensions Service (UK)
MAS	Money Advice Service (UK)
NCA	National Credit Act (SA)
NCR	National Credit Regulator (SA)
Net1	a financial services company (SA)
NGO	non-governmental organization
NHS	National Health Service (UK)
NPM	New Public Management
OCI	Online Compliance Intervention
OPG	older person's grant (SA)
P45	a form titled "details of employee leaving work" providing tax information (UK)
PIP	personal independence payment (UK)
RDP	Reconstruction and Development Programme (SA)

ROSCA rotating savings and credit association

SAfH Social Action for Health (UK)

SAPO South African Post Office (SA)

SASSA South African Social Security Agency (SA)

TC tax credits (UK)

UC universal credit

UEPS Universal Electronic Payment Systems Technologies (see CPS and Net1) (SA)

USLAC University of Stellenbosch Law Clinic (now Stellenbosch University Law Clinic–SULC) (SA)

VAT value-added tax

WTC working tax credit (UK)

A Note on Currency

Since 2015, the South African rand has fluctuated but has been on a downward trend overall.

In 2015, the date of the court case discussed in Chapter 3, R10 = £0.51 or $0.79; R100 = £5.13 or $7.87.

In 2018, the date of the research discussed in Chapter 2, R10 = £0.57 or $0.75; R100 = £5.67 or $7.58.

From 2015–2021, the dates of the research in the UK, the average exchange rate was 1.3; £10 = $1.30; £100 = $130.

CLAWING BACK

INTRODUCTION   Why Redistribution?

ANTHROPOLOGISTS HAVE RECENTLY DEVELOPED an interest in redistribution. In contrast to much of the classic literature, their unique contribution to this study lies in an awareness of how formal and informal redistributive processes interlock. The focus is thus shifting to re-allocative processes beyond those that were tried and tested in the heyday of the welfare state. This book asks how, under these circumstances, people make a living and pay for what they need and want. Where my earlier research focused on the rise of financialized debt, here I bring this topic into conversation with two others. These relate to additional sources of income: wages (in settings where work is becoming more precarious) and welfare payments (increasingly squeezed, diminished, and reduced under conditions of austerity). I also expand the geographical focus by moving beyond South Africa, the topic of my earlier work, to include the United Kingdom. The two settings are linked by colonial history but with few immediately obvious similarities. In both, however, class and inequality are hotly debated. Contradictory processes are at work. While the "new middle class" is said to be expanding—albeit unevenly and often unstably—in the Global South, its members in Euro-America are increasingly devoid of the stable jobs and incomes necessary for a prosperous life.

The book, then, is about redistribution. That said, it is difficult to outline the subject it tackles in a single word, let alone sentence, paragraph, or even chapter. This is because it addresses, and tries to make sense of, a series of phenomena that have not often been seen as connected. Looking across a range of settings, and broadly contrasting a case in the Global South with one in the Global North, it explores the changing economic arrangements through which people have gained access to a livelihood. In addressing questions of financial debt, the book could be seen as concerned with that sub-discipline variously known as economic anthropology or anthropology of economy. But it also explores work and welfare. That is, it asks about the nexus of relationships through which people relate to three sets of actors: the private or state institutions to which (or individuals to whom) they owe money; those who employ them and pay their remuneration; and the government agencies, nongovernmental organizations or charitable institutions through which they might expect social protection. If we view these three interconnected topics through the prism of debt, this affords a very particular and unusual vantage point. Audiences to whom I have presented some of this material are puzzled, often asking me questions that focus on the specificities of debt and sidelining these broader considerations. Why are moneylenders so exploitative—and how is it that this is allowed? Why are borrowers apparently so bad at foreseeing the problems that debt might bring? How can a lending industry be sustainable with such high interest rates? Even more commonly, they suspect—and seek evidence—of how the interests (and profits) of the financialized industries are being pursued by large companies at the expense of the local actors who borrow from them. And, indeed, these are important questions to ask, and to answer.

Why, then, am I arguing that such questions are best understood, instead, as part of a broader vision of redistribution? There are a few interconnected answers, which I will outline simply to begin with. One of them has to do with acknowledging and giving full cognizance to (rather than implicitly deriding) the ubiquitous role of the financial industry. A large proportion of the forms of resource, income, and basic livelihood discussed here are acquired by people borrowing money and accessing loans, rather than being gained through the conventional routes of wage work or social welfare. Or, rather, they are using these means *in addition* to "conventional" routes.

Am I suggesting, then, that financialization and the finance industry are serving a productive, even a beneficial purpose? That would certainly go against the grain of much recent scholarship, in anthropology and beyond. That scholarship shows how, since the 1970s, political and economic processes have been increasingly dominated by finance, as people—including those on the bottom rungs of the social ladder—have taken up products proffered by banks and financial companies. These loans extend beyond those offered by banks (such as insurance products, micro- and student loans, credit card debt, vehicle purchase schemes) to include money lent by retailers (by purchasing on installment) and loan sharks with their informal systems of lending. In the process, those previously unschooled in saving, borrowing, and repaying have been enjoined to become "financially literate" by adapting their uses of money to financial institutions' demands (Krippner 2005, 173–174). The line of argument goes further, arguing that, as political economic processes shifted toward finance, companies' priorities were imprinted on customers and clients, rendering them as "risk-bearing subjects" (Christophers et al. 2017, 27) and fundamentally reshaping their behaviors and subjectivities. Thus was the so-called financialization of daily life accomplished (Martin 2002).

While this line of argument has some validity, I am positing a *different* way of visualizing the relationship between the finance industry and the world of everyday needs, family and household survival, and the relational obligations these might entail. Since lending has become a major way of supplementing income made from other sources—such as wage labor or welfare payments— the way it stands in or substitutes for these sources requires that we see it in a new and somewhat different light. While getting into debt is fraught with risk, it is often one of the few options open to those who are unable to get by with what they earn in wages or what the state may pay them in welfare grants or benefits. But it is not, in many cases, the *only* option: part of the mission of this book is to show how borrowings interweave with the other more—and less—easily recognized re-allocative processes we are used to thinking of when we speak of redistribution. My argument, then, is that debt relations need to be seen not simply, as many have done, as producing a new global culture in which persons are viewed—and view themselves—through a single perspective, as those who repay (or as those who default on repayment). Instead, they need to be understood in relation to other factors—other things that make their search for a viable livelihood possible and that enable their life in society. To restate what I said above, these include interactions with the employers (and/or "the market" or "capital," to phrase it in terms of Marxist political economy) from whom they earn a living. And they also include interactions with the state, from which in some cases, particularly the two under discussion here, they receive various forms of welfare benefit. They also, of course, involve less formal, sometimes less contractual dealings with neighbors and kinsmen. These latter are normally understood to be the bread and butter of anthropological analysis, and I return to them intermittently throughout the book.

A second, related reason for seeing issues of debt in a broader context—as redistribution—involves my using an approach that is more interactionist and agentive than attentive to overall structural patterns. The latter tend to emphasize the broader or higher-level results (and often the overall bleakness) of a world in which low-wage people are pushed into indebtedness. A different perspective, as I will show, has it that the provision of credit enables spaces in which wage earners and householders can find ways to negotiate. Studies of poor householders' responses to financialization often takes a perspective that emphasizes their victim-like status. Even in studies framed in this way, one can read against the grain and find ethnographic examples of how people make use of debt (whether financialized or otherwise) to constitute relations and futures, to engage with the state, to convert between commodified and non-commodified relationships. Such a viewpoint, however, is not a Pollyannaish endorsement of the positive opportunities that borrowing money can bring. Far from it: getting into debt can be dangerous and difficult, requiring vigilance and the necessity constantly to calculate and strategize. Mastering these tactical moves does not equate to "financial literacy" in the bland sense often trotted out by those who try to lecture the poor about the need for frugality. Instead, it involves complex feats of juggling. In some cases people do this in a manner that foregrounds untutored economic culture, local values, and a kind of "self-help." In other cases, somewhat bewildered by both complex welfare bureaucracies and difficult-to-negotiate repayment arrangements, people seek counsel and advice from intermediaries or brokers who stand between them and whatever agency has been cast as providing resources. The work of those who play the latter role, positioned between grassroots borrowers and complex higher-level organizational structures—be they part of state, market, or civil society—forms an important topic of this book.

There is a third reason to conceptualize this terrain in terms of "redistribution." Why *re*distributive? That initial syllable seems to suggest either a repeated action or one that takes into account earlier phases in a sequence. Scholars have spoken of "distribution" and "distributive labor" to evoke the efforts put into building relationships and clientelist ties by those seeking to cultivate and maintain connections. The term conjures up images of (inter) dependence, in contrast to the autonomy of the individual worker earning a wage sufficient for the well-being of her family. "Redistribution," however, suggests not just solidaristic interchange but actual recompense for losses suffered as a result of earlier wrongs. Redistributive impulses are said to have arisen out of a need to counter the inequalities that arise out of the unequal distribution of income and wealth: they are a "tool" to be applied by the state and/or society in order to curb the worst excesses of capitalist exploitation and free trade. Or, in settings where previous political regimes are reformed, or toppled and replaced by new ones, redistribution can be a formal policy specifically aimed at redress. Can we combine notions of reallocation and pay out, on the one hand, with those of compensation for a loss, on the other? If so, we enter a terrain where not only are mechanisms of disbursal in operation, but also where there is a marked expectation of being given back something that was unfairly taken away.

In sum, redistribution can range from high-profile examples such as the shakeup of land ownership in the wake of political change, through less visible/obvious ones like the instantiation or expansion of a welfare regime, to seemingly counterintuitive ones like the extending of credit. The resources disbursed can range from those collected by the state through formal taxation to those assembled through less organized arrangements. It is no longer (if it ever was) just a matter for the state/society; where financialization is accompanied by increased informalization, redistribution can equally involve the market. Or indeed it can draw on—and involve—kinship and social networks. In topographies of wealth flow, funds may move upwards as well as sideways or downwards. Do all such movements count as redistribution? Or does diverting funds away from their intended purpose mean we should think of them in other terms?

Redistribution: Work and Welfare, Finance and Debt

In exploring redistribution, this book brings studies of debt into conversation with the interrelated topics of work and welfare. This means it engages with a domain most often thought of as connected to "social" (in the UK) or "public" (in the US) policy. Such terms are used when discussing the Global North: in southern settings, it is just as often thought of as fitting under the rubric of development. Running the risk of treading on territory already thoroughly traversed by other disciplinary fields, I explore how anthropologists have understood welfare benefits and their relation to the world of work. It is necessary to step (albeit lightly) into this environment—firstly because anthropologists increasingly do their work "at home," including in northern or Euro-American settings where welfare systems have been in existence for more than a century; secondly because of the increasing prevalence of welfare payments, if not full-blown welfare states, in southern settings: "social policy" has emerged as a global phenomenon.[1]

In the terms used by economic historians and other social scientists, the three elements necessary for economic growth are workers, capitalists, and the state (see Freund 2010; Kasmir & Carbonella 2014). If workers and capitalists have had an uneasy and often adversarial relationship, it is the state that has both acted on behalf of capitalists/the market and intervened to ensure that workers are compensated for those disadvantages for which capitalists and the market have been responsible (Elster 1991, 273; Fraser 2014; Therborn 2012, 587). Redistribution, in other words, has been seen as a quintessentially nonmarket, premarket, or antimarket process (see Hann & Hart 2009): one that exists to counter, or offset, the harms caused by the market. Seen in this light, it amounts to compensation by state/society for inequities arising through market processes, often initiated by pressure from workers—and involving taxation.

Economists, although preoccupied (especially in the early years of the modern neoclassical discipline) with the formal logic of how income and wages are determined, and how and whether redistribution might factor in these processes, ultimately concluded that it must come about via ethics or philosophies of justice exterior to economic processes rather than being an intrinsic part of, or deliverable by, economic growth (Sandmo 2015). Redistributive policies, claims Jon Elster in similar vein, "are intended to compensate people for various sorts of bad luck, arising mainly in the market" (1991, 273): a market that, although it may promote growth, also leads to exploitation and inequality—and these require remedy (Fraser 2014, 547). Putting it more strongly, Göran Therborn (2012, 587) writes of how "redistribution and recompensation are powerful tools," arising largely out of the struggles of the labor movement, through which "remedial action" can be undertaken to counter the egregious inequalities that arise out of the unequal distribution of income and wealth. Such "tools," it is claimed, must be applied by society and/or the state in order to curb the worst excesses of capitalist exploitation and free trade. As Chris Hann and Keith Hart put it, "the leading capitalist societies at one stage all signed up for Hegel's (1821) idea that states should try to contain the inequality and ameliorate the social misery generated by markets" (2009, 2).

From these underpinnings, in post-war Europe, was the welfare state born. That is, redistributive social welfare systems involve nonmarket initiatives and institutions counteracting the iniquities produced by the market, especially by exploitative labor relations. But they have taken new shape. Initially developed in northern European and North American metropoles, their scope was intentionally restricted to those contexts and denied to people living in more peripheral settings, including those northern countries had colonized (Cooper 1997). They have since significantly shrunk or mutated in their original heartlands while simultaneously diffusing and proliferating in formerly colonized and/or more "peripheral" countries (but often in emaciated form). Workers have been increasingly excluded from formal, state-run redistributive schemes or have found themselves pushed towards those in which the market has primacy.

The welfare state, invented by the Bismarck government in late nineteenth-century Germany, post-unification (Chang 2022; Clark 2007), centered on workers' rights, but was designed less to enshrine radical-style worker politics than to contain these and, in the process, to undermine support for socialism (Esping-Andersen 1990, 15). Later models were developed in the US, with Roosevelt's New Deal, and in the UK, with Beveridge's post-war welfare state. They encompassed a universalist vision of social security, education, and healthcare for all, including the unemployed. From the end of World War II, and for the following thirty years, the outcome of labor struggles—to put it simply—saw workers' rights in the more prosperous Western countries buttressed and the well-being of those without work simultaneously assured. Nevertheless, anthropologists and others have cautioned that the welfare state was "the exception rather than the norm, even in Europe" (Sanchez & Lazar 2019).

If that is so, what about countries from the Global South? These were linked to metropoles by histories of rights and entitlements alternately demanded and refused. Metropolitan governments, recognizing that establishing European-style welfare states in these colonies was hardly feasible, withdrew. This recognition, in part, was what prompted their "granting" of independence—in seemingly cynical mode—to these colonies (Cooper 1997; Fraser 2014, 553–554).[2] But, despite these strategic maneuverings, systems of social welfare did take root in other settings. These were often fashioned, at least in part, on Euro-American models. In South Africa, for example, the 1930s saw the development of a robust welfare system to address problems of poverty during the Depression. Inspired by a report funded by the Carnegie

Foundation, however, it was racially skewed, addressing the "poor white" problem in particular and initially excluding the majority of the population, notably those black workers, mostly migrants, on whose labor South Africa's mining industry depended (Breckenridge 2014; Ferguson 2015; Seekings 2020). Later, the biometric systems on which this welfare bureaucracy relied provided a framework for including black pensioners, and later still a range of grants for child support grants (Breckenridge 2014, 181–187) and eventually, post-democracy, for the roll-out of "social grants" (Ferguson 2015; Fouksman & Dawson 2024; Webb & Mgijima 2024). In Brazil until 1988, it was the Bismarckian model of welfare, involving "rights deriving from the status of employee" and "associated with formal work," that prevailed (Georges 2024). The later development of a Beveridgian model—and eventually a cash transfer system—in Brazil saw *citizen* rather than *worker* rights take center stage (Georges 2024; Lavinas 2018). In both cases, and in many others in the Global South, support, although more universal in being extended to those beyond the workplace, was also narrower. It often consisted mainly of cash transfers and excluded the comprehensive provision of services (Olivier de Sardan & Piccoli 2018).[3]

In many settings in the Global South, then, welfare systems were never fully developed. Delivering welfare in the form of cash payments or transfers makes individual recipients responsible for its use in funding their own life beyond the wage. Since such payments are often inadequate, this leaves recipients with few options but to borrow from purveyors of short-term, high-interest loans (Han 2012; James 2015) or have their welfare payments repurposed as loan collateral (James et al. 2020; Lavinas 2018; Torkelson 2020). Welfare has, in the process, started to morph into "debtfare" (Krippner 2017; Soederberg 2014). Meanwhile, if welfare payments are indeed compensations for the inadequacies of workers' wages and for problems arising out of the prevalence of market mechanisms, as posited by scholars like Göran Therborn and Nancy Fraser, what are we to make of settings where work seems ever scarcer? It is here that questions of work, welfare, and debt intersect most visibly.

To claim that these three areas are inextricably interwoven seems, on the face of it, to be arguing against the grain. It counters important claims about the decline of wage labor. Writing about post-democracy South Africa, James Ferguson (2015) argues that the sovereign subject whose well-being is predicated on labor is being eclipsed by the non-sovereign one with a life centered on dependency. Rather than trying to squeeze more and more people into an ever-smaller category of the employed, a new politics of distribution—involving cash transfers or basic income grants—would, he claims, enable a world of well-being based on an acceptance of such dependency, accompanied by political demands for the "fair share."[4] Similarly, writing with Tanya Murray Li, he maintains that expectations of ever-expanding wage employment and of "the proper job" are misleading and have lost plausibility as a universal solution (Ferguson & Li 2018). It is certainly the case, as argued by various anthropologists, that work in the Global South has "always-already" been precarious (Parry 2018; Sanchez & Lazar 2019). As structural adjustment or austerity policies have been implemented, as immaterial and intermittent labor became prevalent, as firms moved abroad, and/or as value was extracted from labor well beyond the wage relation (Casas-Cortès 2017, cited in Sanchez & Lazar 2019, 4), life has in some cases become increasingly "wageless" (Denning 2010). Hardly more encouraging are cases where dependence on wages has deepened as workers have found themselves compelled to work overtime in order to keep body and soul together (Luong & Nguyen 2024).[5]

These changes—the global trend towards precarity, more casualization, greater dependence on family and other networks (Parry 2018, 14)—appear, in all kinds of settings, to have turned back the advances made, through worker struggles, to advance social protection and welfare. State-provided redistribution and security appear to become an ever-remoter prospect, disappearing rapidly into the rearview mirror of history. Yet even those who seem to have no alternative but to build an independent livelihood out of various fragments, creating "portfolios of social protection" (Nguyen 2020) or relying on what Caitlin Zaloom and I call "patchworks" of funds (2023), have not abandoned visions of a world where wages and welfare exist and can be relied upon. At the same time, neither workers nor those solely on welfare benefits are able to get by without borrowing money, using loans made increasingly available as a result of the expansion of finance into everyday life.

I turn, then, to a brief discussion of debt, exploring its intersection with these other terms in my triangle of income sources. Ordinary people, often those never previously able to borrow, are increasingly in debt. The processes that have enabled so-called financial inclusion by those formerly without bank accounts have also, in parallel, facilitated accelerated access to credit. These processes have been characterized as premised on "financialization." From the creditor's point of view, this means a new "pattern of accumulation in which profits accrue primarily through financial channels rather than through trade and commodity production" while from the borrower's perspective it involves confrontation with "new financial products" (Krippner 2005, 174). These, in their more formal guise, are offered by banks and governments, but they are also available from retailers and loan sharks in the shape of install-ment purchasing, payday loans, or borrowing from relatives. Those previously unschooled in saving, borrowing, and repaying are enjoined to become "fi-nancially literate" and required to adapt their uses of money to financial in-stitutions' demands (Krippner 2005, 173–174). Financialization, in this book, mainly equates to the expanded use of loans and other financial products by households in provisioning kin and aspiring to social advancement (Zaloom & James 2023). But these are not, or not always, their only source of income.

Accompanying these developments, financial institutions and even some anthropologists have come to accept a basic division as foundational. This division bifurcates experience: it "separates a formalized, often professional, financial sphere from one of intimate relations and depends upon a partition of commodified and non-commodified relationships" (Zaloom & James 2023). Some anthropological examinations of finance and of households have tended to reproduce this binary thinking, seeing economy and family as separate and deducing that the former—especially after the rapid rise of financializing pro-cesses in the last few decades of the twentieth century—influences the latter in hegemonic fashion. They chart the rapid increase in borrowing in both northern and southern settings and note the intensifying reliance on finance by corporations and governments, both to make profit and to govern and pro-vision populations and shape behavior. Many then conclude that, "as political economic processes shifted toward finance, social life followed" (Zaloom & James 2023). They also point to the way that citizens, subjects, customers, and clients have been rendered as "risk-bearing subjects" (Christophers et al. 2017, 27), and even to the way that the credit-debt relation has replaced or super-seded all others (Lazzarato 2012).

Other anthropologists (and I count myself among their number) consider, however, that this top-down approach distorts matters, firstly by assuming that financialized capitalism is the uniformly dominant partner in this pair-ing, and secondly by accepting as given the boundedness and separation of distinct spheres: economy and household. An alternative approach is to recog-nize "how widespread instruments of finance lock together with closely-held systems of obligation and visions of prosperity that structure kin relations," and show how, while "familial and financial spheres may appear separate,

. . . exchanges between them constitute and remake one another" (Zaloom & James 2023). Pursuing this line of argument means viewing things from the point of view of the (debtor) householders who increasingly make use of loans and other financial products. Such people can use these to their own ends (Guérin 2014; Guérin & Kumar 2020; Webb & Mgijima 2024), even when the cards seem to be stacked against them. Anthropological analysis, then, "does not presume to know the outcome of financialization; instead, it . . . advances arguments about the social reconfigurations financial encounters produce," as Caitlin Zaloom and I have argued, in order to succeed in "caring for kith, kin, and self" (Zaloom & James 2023). Householders thrown up on the peripheries of—but still contributing through their labor to—global capitalist arrangements may thus exercise some control over their social relations and life projects. They do so not despite, but because of, their involvement with the market, commodification of life, and finance.

"Economic" Life and the Broker: An Agentive Approach

Asking questions about income, exchange, and the accumulation and dispersal of wealth takes us squarely into the terrain that has come to be called "anthropology of economy." At the time of writing, in 2022, the anthropological community had just celebrated the centenary of Bronislaw Malinowski's 1922 book *Argonauts of the Western Pacific*. Several of those attending a workshop at LSE[6] followed up on Malinowski's initial line of inquiry by asking searching questions. Just because production, exchange, and consumption in the Trobriands were regulated by custom, magic, and kinship, they reminded us, this did not mean that islanders weren't mindful of more rational-sounding economic motivations. This was noted by Malinowski himself, and the gaps between the former (elements that sound more socially embedded) and the latter (which comprise what we now think of as economic) have formed a core puzzle for anthropological thinking ever since. Or, to reverse the syntax, just because production, exchange, and consumption in the Trobriands involved rational-sounding economic motivations, this did not mean that islanders were not governed by custom, magic, and kinship (Hann & James 2024).

But, had Malinowski's ideas been taken more seriously in the first place, we might have ended up with a different idea of what "economic" means. Malinowski's paper published in *The Economic Journal* in the same year as *Argonauts* (1922), makes it clear how the primary methods of anthropology and neoclassical economics diverged in this period, with the latter taking an individualistically psychological and deductive approach. The implication is that "economic" explanations—which as the century progressed ended up moving ever further in the direction of calculative rationality—should actually have been seen as integrally connected to "non-economic" ones—which, in many cases, were gradually hiving off into a separate zone of "culture." Had these two approaches not diverged, the main stream of economic thinking might have proceeded differently, in a more holistic direction.

We might add a further important element of Malinowski's thinking into the mix. This is his famous (and much-criticized) aversion to considering Durkheim-style overarching structures, and his preference—while describing and analyzing shared patterns of behavior in society—for looking at individual action in a manner that foregrounded calculative logic and seemed crudely "empiricist" (Leach 1957). In *Culture and Practical Reason*, Marshall Sahlins described his approach, highlighting individual motivations, as "utilitarian functionalism" and said, dismissively, that "the content is appreciated only for its instrumental effect, and its internal consistency is thus mystified as its external utility" (1976, 76). For scholars favoring Weberian approaches, more strongly embedded in the "culture" than the "practical reason" of Sahlins's title, it became increasingly problematic to favor the latter approach with its foregrounding of the calculative and maximizing individual.

Yet it is the reintroduction of that individual agent that I seek, in a certain measure, to achieve here. It is that agent, surrounded by her household and family members and with her own logics—which may be calculative and relational by turn, but which are not wholly determined by the structures of global capitalism—whose stories form the substance of this book. She may never be driven solely by profit or "practical reason"—motives on which, said these critical scholars, Malinowski focused too much. Indeed, since she may never be separated from others as a pure and isolated individual (if such a thing exists), her actions may be equally guided by culture. But neither should her actions be seen as the automatic outcome of profiteering decisions made by those in boardrooms and CEOs' offices.

Converging with this area of debate is the question of how intermediaries or brokers bridge the gaps that otherwise exist between divergent social settings or individuals. These are specific (often idiosyncratic, even opportunistic) agents that emerge or arise in the interstices between larger forces. Lest this interest on brokers sound naively focused on the actions of specific individuals, we should be attentive to a claim by Anne-Meike Fechter, who shows that they are "located between fault lines and connection points within complex systems and relationships." What requires but also enables brokerage, in particular, are increasing relations of inequality and "of decentralisation" (2020, 295–296).

In my earlier work on this, I have stressed how different and unevenly blended elements not only provide the context in which brokers emerge, but also furnish the bricoleurs' hybrid toolkit on which they draw: combining apparently divergent discourses or modalities of being, they are not only products, but also producers, of the kind of society in which they emerge. The broker serves to create and perpetuate such conditions, embodies the contradictions that ensue, and operates to mediate these. In a setting where the state intervenes, partly to create conditions where the market will have primacy but also to ameliorate the resulting inequities through redistributive practices, such brokers can play crucial roles (James 2011).

What relevance does this have for formal and informal redistributive systems? What role might brokers play in helping to claw back debtors' owings in an attempt to protect them? Or should these kinds of intermediaries leave well alone, trusting in the kinds of self-help strategies and negotiations outlined in Chapters 1 and 2? In the case of formal measures, Elster reminds us that "globally redistributive policies" that are "designed centrally, at the level of the national government" often require the intervention of "second-order decision makers" to ensure that "local justice" is in fact done (Elster 1991, 273). Those offering free, state-funded advice in the UK, for example (see Chapters 4 and 5), are committed to mastering bureaucratic techniques of allocation and to implementing these in line with the redistributive spirit that is presumed to have animated their original design, no matter how much these may subsequently have been diverted or interrupted by austerity measures. In the case of less formal ones, such intermediaries may be equally essential. Advice in South Africa is more sporadic and funded more intermittently, but part of the work of Black Sash aimed at remedying this lack.

Let us return to Malinowski and the Trobriands. What might a socially embedded, agentive account of economy look like, if we applied it to contexts far more modernized and far more integrated into a capitalist system than 1920s Papua New Guinea—one where people's lives seem to be partly or wholly determined by powerful outside forces? Could such an account give us novel insights into how people use, share, or view their income—whether it be borrowed, earned, or allocated? What, in short, are the implications of this for a new understanding of redistribution?

Between the perhaps crudely overstated market-driven calculative motives attributed to the Trobrianders by Malinowski and the more embedded agency that I try to introduce here, there have been a multitude of intervening debates, with numerous assumptions and variables. There has been intense discussion over how economic and non-economic relate, with many scholars misunderstanding their predecessors and others accusing them, in turn, of wrong-footedness. Marcel Mauss, for example, using Malinowski's work in *Essai sur le Don* (2016), has often been seen as depicting a total division between "our world" based on market principles and an ideal earlier world based on altruism. But this teleological interpretation has been challenged. Mauss, says Hart, was showing that *both* impulses—utilitarian interest and socially embedded reciprocity—may be present in any kind of social order (Hart 2007). Our discussions at the 2022 workshop suggested that Malinowski's writings could themselves be interpreted in a similar vein.

There is one oeuvre, recently somewhat neglected within the economic anthropology tradition, on which I draw in the book. This is the early work of Clifford Geertz. In his book *Peddlers and Princes* (1968), he grappled explicitly with the transition to modern economic growth in Indonesia, depicting two contrasting instances of adaptation to capitalist-style accumulation. In both, but in contrasting ways, existing sociocultural affordances enable that adaptation while also hampering it. For the peddlers in Modjokuto, their affiliation to pietistic Islamic religion means they are disconnected from the social ties that might put the brakes on their enterprise, but their very isolation from broader structures means they lack the support that might have enabled their firms to grow. For the princes in Tabanan, their social embeddedness gives them relationships through which they endeavor to reorganize the town's economic system, but their traditionalism impedes any real accumulation of capital because these very obligations pressurize them to redistribute resources rather than investing them. The conclusion drawn by Geertz, with his then interest in economic change and enterprise, is that Modjokuto firms fail to grow while Tabanan's fail to rationalize. Both "peddler" and "prince" mentalities need to be dispensed with, to be replaced by that of "the professional manager," he claims: a somewhat pro-business-sounding stance that his later interpretive work did not pursue.

The people who appear in my book, unlike Geertz's peddlers and princes, are not would-be entrepreneurs. They are borrowers, laborers, and welfare beneficiaries—often all three at once—who find themselves at the sharp end of financialized processes, restructured workplaces, and shrinking forms of social protection. And, in their search to secure an income through various redistributive means, they seek help from, and enter interactions with, human rights lawyers, NGO officers, and debt advisers: a second set of economic agents whose activities are discussed in these pages. Despite these differences, it remains the case that, for them as for Geertz's interlocutors, individualizing agency is inseparably entangled with, or dependent for its actualization on, social relationships. But that agency is neither buried in, nor altogether effaced by, these relationships. Nor are their actions wholly determined by overarching structural forces—whether of financiers, industry, or the state. Instead, they are protagonists of what Zaloom calls "enmeshed autonomy" (2019; see Chapter 5). Had Malinowski's original contribution succeeded in pointing the way towards a different understanding of "economic," the calculative/maximizing and the relational/reciprocal aspects—and indeed agency and structure—might have been folded together in a more holistic way. Such an approach can have important implications for how we view redistribution.

Redistribution: Clawing Back What We Had Before?

"Clawing back" is an evocative metaphor. It suggests vigorous and determined effort to regain a lost position or advantage. It captures an important aspect of the actions and practices described in this book. These are actions taken by ordinary people, whether wage earners, borrowers, or welfare recipients, or their adviser/representatives, to get what they feel is theirs—to achieve fair play.

The small-scale and local-level initiatives discussed here may, however, seem too piecemeal and fragmented to merit a grand term such as "redistribution." They appear far less ambitious than the visionary schemes advanced by Ferguson in his 2015 book *Give a Man a Fish*. That book advocates for welfare systems, like the unconditional BIG (basic income grant) originally proposed for South Africa but not so far implemented there, that distribute cash and leave beneficiaries to decide on its use. In the final chapter of Ferguson's book, while duly acknowledging the technical difficulties of finding an effective mechanism for distributing such transfers, he nonetheless makes a persuasive case. He says that the chances of giving all a job are slim and should not be relied upon; that cash transfers or grants have brought some relief (even some plenty and enjoyment); and giving them out might point the way forward to a new, emergent form of politics. Such a politics might, simultaneously, embrace two seemingly contradictory impulses. One is that, shorn of conditionalities and obligations to earn a wage, workless people have an acknowledged dependency on the state or the wider polity for their "rightful share"; the other is the autonomy through which beneficiaries decide for themselves how best to deploy and plan for the use of that "share."

The resonances and utopian-sounding promises of Ferguson's book (2015, 187–189) seem to foreshadow other recent discourses centered on the reintroduction of some form of commons (Muehlebach 2023; Philipsen 2021). Some have arisen in the context of debates on climate change and the need for degrowth. In a review article, Geoff Mann (2022) discusses *The Case for Degrowth* by Giorgos Kallis and co-authors (2020). He shows how they make the case for "limiting the reach of private property relations and reviving 'commoning' practices or distributing technologies and financial support as reparations for the legacies of colonialism in the Global South" (Mann 2022, 29). Like Ferguson, however, he points out that it is not clear "who or what body has the political power to make all this happen" (Mann 2022, 29). In the absence of ambitious and overarching schemes, I attend to the ways in which workers, borrowers, and/or welfare recipients—and those who provide them with advice—battle to secure the welfare that is due to them. In the process I explore the emerging folk models of fiscal behavior or householding that emerge.

One might query the validity of such an exercise. Surely the global spread of financialized techniques involves transnational corporations, uses standardized technologies of extraction, and must have a uniformly deleterious (and broadly homogenizing) effect worldwide. It is not my intention to present an idealized image of forms of support that transcend the stark realities of capitalist exploitation, nor to flatly deny the claims of scholars in a neo-Marxist or Foucauldian tradition who are inclined to see activists, advisers, and/or volunteers as doing the state's work by providing momentary redress and protection against the worst effects of capitalism or austerity (Davey 2022; see Koch & James 2022). Rather, my account is motivated by a recognition that activities within or at the boundaries of formal processes, whether initiated or funded by the state or by commercial companies or simply accomplished through self-help, can mitigate and counter the exclusion of poorer people (Kirwan et al. 2016). It is also motivated by ideas about "care ethics" that move us "beyond critique and toward the construction of new forms of relationships, institutions, and action that enhance mutuality and well-being" (Lawson 2007).

Researching Redistribution

But do these count as redistribution? In the two fieldwork settings explored here, which track developments over more than a decade, activities aimed at clawing back resources certainly have some resonances with this idea.[7] The first is that of post-apartheid South Africa, whose encounter with debt and credit I have been exploring since 2007 (James 2015, 2017a, 2017b, 2021). The second is austerity Britain between 2015 and 2021, where I was involved in a collaborative study—in particular with Alice Forbess, as seen in Chapters 4 and 5—of debt and welfare advice (Forbess & James 2014, 2017; James 2020, 2022a; James & Kirwan 2019; Koch & James 2022). Attempting—at the end of all this—a comparative framing to pick out commonalities and differences between the two settings, as well as viewing changes within each of them over time, I have drawn selectively on some of this already-published work, as well as using new ethnographic and documentary materials gathered more recently. Notably, in 2017 I conducted interviews and investigated the files from a groundbreaking court case concerning creditors' use of garnishee orders, which form the basis of Chapter 3, while in 2018–19 I was involved in a collaborative research project with South African NGO Black Sash, investigating the use of social grants as loan collateral, which yielded an unpublished document containing the case studies gathered by all three authors (James et al. n.d.) and a report published in 2020 (James et al. 2020). These form the basis of discussions in Chapters 1 and 2, respectively. In both these cases, but in different ways over the ensuing decade, people (and sometimes their advisers) have been involved in intensive efforts at getting enough to live on and even to progress, but also at resisting extractive demands on them to make excessive repayments when debts fall due.

Redistribution in its more politicized sense was certainly in evidence in the South African case. Those previously disadvantaged, or kept in the lower ranks of the workforce, were clamoring to join the wider society and get compensation or redress for what had earlier been denied. But all this was happening against the backdrop of intense disputes about the nature of the new order: would it be broadly socialist in orientation, as elements within the formerly

exiled ANC were demanding, or would liberalization or neoliberal capitalism prevail? As these disputes were going on, I began to study how forms of
economic inclusion or redress were playing out in the lives of individuals—
specifically, efforts to overcome "credit apartheid," that is, to extend the right
to borrow to those largely denied it in the past by the racially discriminatory
social order. The dynamics surrounding South Africa's national project of financial inclusion, which aimed to extend credit to black South Africans as a
crucial aspect of broad-based economic enfranchisement, turned out to be
contradictory. Many of those who were attempting to improve their positions
(or merely sustain their existing livelihoods) were able to do so only by turning
to borrowing. This proved necessary, given what was happening at the level of
the nation and of industry. The rapid liberalization of the economy meant a
decline in industrial and other types of employment, and "jobless growth"
meant money was being made chiefly through finance (and informal borrowing and lending). While access to credit delivered to many the prosperity they
had hoped for, obligations to repay—and anxiety about failing to do so—took
their toll. They struggled against such obligations when they were unfair and
found ways to counter these. Both borrowing and reactions against its unforeseen consequences—clawbacks—had a redistributive edge (James 2015, 2017).

As noted earlier, the making of South Africa's earlier welfare system had
been linked to the enforced segregation of apartheid: the more the Afrikaner
poor were included, the more the black poor were not. (In other African settings, the only real provisions made were those aimed at stabilizing a more
middle-class group, rather than at providing a safety net for the African poor
(Ferguson 2015, 71–73).) Exploring why, in post-democracy South Africa, the
tide suddenly turned and wider provision was made, Ferguson proposes two
chief reasons. First, there was a realization that rural livelihoods had de-
clined. Second, recognizing that it had failed to produce "robust employment
growth," the new ANC government was obliged to furnish some kind of safety
net. This it did through the provision of cash transfers (2015, 78).

In the UK case, the notion of redistribution was similarly evident, albeit in
more muted form. Rising unemployment, deskilling of industrial work, and
an increase in precarious jobs had already been underway when the global
financial crisis of 2007–2008 occurred. The newly elected Coalition government, under a Conservative fiscal regime, adopted a policy of austerity measures. Initiatives to introduce compensation for this regressive process was a
response—a kind of "double movement." (This phrase, coined by Karl Polanyi

(1944), refers to the push for social protection that follows as a consequence of, and reaction against, the effects of marketization and commodification.) Severe cuts to welfare benefits—and also to the advice services needed to access these—were made in the name of the contradictorily labeled "welfare reform." This resulted in an unprecedented wave of borrowing and indebtedness, but cutbacks to advice services were making it more difficult to get counsel on how to deal with the negative effects (James & Koch 2020).

Despite cuts in funding, indebted people and those counseling them managed to push back. Some found new resource flows, piecing them together to form new patchworks of funds. Driven by complex motivations that included paternalistic empathy and careerism, advisers found ways of helping clients to deal with commercial debts and to pay their rent, council, and other tax, while challenging the incorrect and unfair reclaiming of benefits (Forbess & James 2017). Here, one kind of alleged reform, done in the name of enhanced efficiency and eliminating fraud but ultimately aimed at recommodifying welfare (see Esping-Andersen 1990), was being countered by something one might more aptly term "reform," in which groups in civil society and householders alike were pushing back against a state whose fiscal arrangements were causing them harm. This countermovement echoed a longer-term historical pattern in Britain, where "reform is often understood as something which is the outcome of public agitation against an at-best-reluctant government" (Cunningham 1998).

In settings where the hegemonic powers of capitalism seem to be operating unchecked, and where more ambitious re-instantiations of the welfare state or more radical reconfigurations of lending regimes seem destined to run into the sand, people find creative ways to combine wages, grants, and borrowings. They are aided by agents who pool their knowledge, providing evidence for legal action in order to push back against unjust demands, or who help their clients make sense of their income by parsing it and separating obligations from optative spending. In both settings, redistributive impulses go hand in hand with ideas about sustainable householding. In South Africa, a recent democratic transition, combined with financial liberalization, has seen a decline (but not disappearance) of wage work, intensified reliance on cash transfers, and an increase in borrowing. Despite the difficulty of reversing a longstanding tendency to extractivism, now in heavily financialized form, hybrid private/corporate actors have combined with government initiatives, functioning to curb the otherwise untrammeled activities of lenders. Here, "householding" means seeking to reclaim appropriated funds while tirelessly working to challenge, often in court, those who ransack pay packets and bank accounts. In the UK, austerity policies mean that government agencies are withdrawing what was previously, in the heyday of the welfare state, publicly funded and seen as a right. People are encouraged to turn to increasingly fragile casual (or zero-hours contract) employment rather than relying on benefits, while also being pushed to practice frugality and to economize.[8] Advisers both facilitate and also contrive to undermine these agendas. Here, "householding" means maximizing income from dwindling sources and challenging repayment obligations.

Investigating redistribution, the book shows how financial demands are received, responded to, and transformed when incorporated into collective life. It shows how householders, rather than acceding helplessly to the demands of more powerful forces, cobble together resources from hybrid sources to achieve their own objectives.

Chapter Outline

Chapter 1 uses examples from South Africa and the UK to explore the interaction between the triad of elements—debt, work, and welfare. It views debt as part of this complex matrix. Rather than a single-stranded phenomenon that, as an outcome of financialization, has turned welfare into debtfare and welfare beneficiaries into repayors, it takes debt (in relation to other, broader factors) to make a viable livelihood possible for such people and to enable their life in society. They make a living by borrowing money and accessing loans *in addition* to the conventional routes of state benefits and wage labor. But, because their circumstances are often such that the unexpected and often unpredictable immediacies of the present make long-term planning difficult, they grapple with the differentiated temporalities of the credit cycle by using tactics other than rational-seeming budgeting strategies.

Chapter 2, focusing on the South African case, further challenges prevalent approaches to financialization, in which binary thinking about the stark separation of commodified and non-commodified relationships is prevalent, market logics intrude into intimate family and social relations, and families are disciplined to act in ways that reproduce the formalized demands of financial contracts. Recipients of welfare may use the money they borrow both to pay for health care or transport, but also to invest in social well-being (especially through savings clubs) rather than purely its economic equivalent. For these people, both debt itself, and attempts to ameliorate its most egregious effects, can be analyzed as forms of redistribution.

Chapter 3, again focusing on the South African case, explores a ground-breaking case in which the right to deduct debt repayments from workers' wages was successfully challenged in the courts. Using evidence from case files and interviews with the lawyers concerned, it discusses how the wages of people in the low-paid sector—farm workers, cleaners, supermarket shelf-packers, and the like—had become subject to automatic subtractions. But these wage deductions have, at the same time, been a site of contestation, in which various protagonists have sought to activate "counter-deductions." In the protracted legal battle, a public interest law clinic assembled, and pro-duced in evidence, paper files, electronic data, and other forms of lists. As the intensity of the struggle ramped up, it also turned out to be a struggle over how much of a worker's wage is "enough" and whether the deductions were constitutional.

Chapter 4 moves on to discuss the UK where, in contrast to South Africa, a robust advice sector helps those in trouble with debt and/or welfare. Although this is partly state funded, it is also the case that a mixed economy of welfare, prevalent for more than a century in the funding and administering of social protection, has become even more dominant in recent times. This involves a pluralist hybrid of market, non-market (e.g., redistribution by the welfare state), and non-monetary (based on reciprocity) forms of economy. Advisers situated at the interstices of these different sectors deploy their expertise and mediatory abilities—aiding clients in sifting through the complex bureaucra-cies involved in accessing state welfare funds or in crafting agile responses to demands for (often excessive) repayments from creditors. By guiding strapped families through financial possibilities, they also establish distinctions among the sources they draw together, thus categorizing resources and assigning them as belonging to either households, governments, banks, or others. They, and the organizations in which they work, are also crucially involved in stitch-ing together the "patches" from novel sources that must be relied on as state backing is increasingly withdrawn. While this involves similar processes of boundary maintenance, since each stream of funding comes with a specific designation and set of conditionalities, it also requires an ability to combine these fragments for pragmatic or performative effect.

Chapter 5, returning to consider both the UK and South Africa comparatively, is particularly concerned with the increasing use of automated "techno-political" systems to recover debts and to turn debtors into fiscal citizens. It focuses in particular on a setting in the UK (Australia also features) where the state often looms larger as creditor than do banks or credit card companies. Householders receive money in advance but, with increasing frequency, are required to repay a large sum at a future time: a phenomenon known as "overpayments." Since repayments are often secured in automated fashion by deducting them from future payments, debt collection poses few problems for the creditor/state, but it would leave welfare recipients in the lurch without the intervention of advisers. Family members are unlikely to achieve true self-sufficiency nor are they able to achieve independent book-balancing. Instead, their situation is one of "enmeshed autonomy" (Zaloom 2019). In interaction with advisers, they accomplish the "relational work" (Zelizer 2012) that is necessary to make overpayment demands intelligible.

ONE

Debt, Work, and Welfare

IN 2015, A SOUTH AFRICAN newspaper reported on the circumstances of Akhona, a domestic cleaner, who was reliant on a mixture of a wage, state welfare, and loans. "Sometimes I only get paid R1,800 [about $142 or £98] a month," she was reported as saying. "And it's not enough because transport is expensive and I have to buy household things, and support other family members." Supplementing her wage as a part-time worker were a monthly child-support grant from the state welfare agency, amounting to R640 at the time. She also relied on a monthly amount of R200, which she routinely borrowed from a company called Moneyline: a sum that she set aside to pay the cost of getting to work. Repayments each month to Moneyline (which is a subsidiary of the agency that distributed the grants) were being made automatically by deductions from those grant payments, with an interest rate of 5 percent.[1]

In 2017, in the UK, a woman called Victoria, a healthcare assistant, told her London debt adviser of a set of strategies that, although vastly different in scale, in some ways resembled Akhona's approach. She was paying her rent and some bills from her monthly salary of £1,500 and using two credit cards for her other expenses: one to buy groceries and the other for transport. She was paying off £130 on each of them—£260 in total per month. The total amount she owed on these was about £10,000. She was not, as yet, in receipt of any state welfare: "If you are used to working, you don't think of claiming benefits," she told the adviser. But she was being counseled about the need to claim whichever of these she was entitled to, which included housing benefit, working tax credits, and some remission of council tax.[2]

Although these two cases are worlds apart in many respects, what they have in common is their reliance, as a partial means to provision livelihood, on the credit that has become more readily available over the past few decades. The expansion of the welfare state in southern settings like South Africa, via the provision of cash transfers, and its shrinking or curtailment in northern settings (coupled in both cases with the rising cost of living), seem to have led inexorably—albeit in different ways—to an increase in borrowing. In Euro-America, the basics of education, healthcare, and housing that were formerly promised by the state are now left to individuals (Brown 2015; Langley 2009) or families (Cooper 2014; Zaloom 2019) to secure for themselves. Since those of modest or limited means are unable to afford such an outlay, lenders and governments have established or extended programs offering credit, tax incentives, and investment vehicles (Kalb 2020; Lapavitsas 2013; see Zaloom & James 2023). Many people—not only the poor or unemployed but also workers on low to middling levels of pay—have thus been brought into the ambit of, or "enfolded within," formal financialized arrangements (Kar 2018). These developments have been analyzed as marking a major transformation. Welfare has become "debtfare"—increased reliance of the poor on credit to augment or replace their wages (Soederberg 2014). Welfare beneficiaries, as support is cut back, have become repayors of debt (Adkins 2017). Coinciding with an increased reliance by both corporations and governments on finance as a strategy for profitmaking and for governing, provisioning their populations, and shaping their behavior, this change has also been seen as signaling a sociocultural shift towards the "financialization of daily life" (see Zaloom & James 2023).

These points are certainly accurate in broad outline. But it is the argument of this chapter that they tell only a portion of the story. In it, I explore a triad of elements—debt, work, and welfare—as they interact in two contexts: South Africa and the UK. Seeing debt as part of this complex matrix, rather than as a single-stranded phenomenon that is the outcome of financialization, enables a new perspective. While the chapter certainly evidences "the expanded use of loans and other financial products by households in provisioning kin and aspiring to social advancement" (Zaloom & James 2023), it transcends claims that "daily life" (Martin 2002) or "everyday life" (Lazarus 2020; Saiag 2020; van der Zwan 2014) has become a wholly-owned subsidiary of financial companies. Looking at the way low-income families, in particular, use loans in partial provision of livelihoods also helps us rise above simplistic claims about their encounter with new financial products. The use of these products—here especially automatic-repayment loans, payday loans, and informal borrowing—does not necessarily lead to, or involve, the financially literate responses that financial institutions aim to impose (Krippner 2005, 173–174; Zaloom 2019, 48–49). If householders refrain from using rational-sounding budgeting strategies, this is because their circumstances are often such that the unexpected and often unpredictable immediacies of the present make long-term planning utopian at best and unthinkable at worst.

It is thus too simple to argue that welfare has changed seamlessly to debt-fare and that former welfare beneficiaries have been transformed into repayors. Firstly, as these two vignettes illustrate and as countless other examples similarly testify, many indebted people are also dependent on—or anticipate getting access to—forms of redistribution furnished by the state, and in addition are earning a (partial) income through work. They make a living by borrowing money and accessing loans *in addition* to the conventional routes of state benefits and wage labor. Debt relations thus need to be seen, not simply as producing persons who are indebted, repayors, or defaulters on repayment. Instead, they need to be understood in relation to other, broader factors that make their search for a viable livelihood possible and that enable their life in society. (One must of course take seriously, however, the claims made by debt advisers and legal and human rights advocates that—notwithstanding the benefits that loans may furnish—the high interest rates attached especially to small and unsecured loans ultimately result in hardship and are unsustainable.)

Secondly, the depiction of an inexorable and quasi-automatic transformation of life by processes of financialization obscures an important factor. It denies the involvement and agency of those affected, rendering them as victims at best and willing (if unknowing) colluders at worst. Thirdly, as will be discussed in Chapters 3 and 4, it is inaccurate to dismiss market (and specifically financial) actors as causing the harms that redistribution is charged with remedying. Institutions of financialized capitalism, even as some of their agents (and logics) plunge people further into debt, have also provided the means to ensure, or at least do not foreclose on the possibility of ensuring, that welfare beneficiaries secure some benefits. In the process, welfare arrangements have been mediated but are not erased altogether.

Distributional or Wage Labor?

James Ferguson, as already noted in the Introduction, is critical of scholarly approaches centered on wage labor and preoccupied with the political actions of the proletariat. He suggests that these are increasingly irrelevant or inapplicable. Instead, we should focus on what he calls "distributional labor" (2015, 2019; see Ferguson & Li 2018). I turn here to the relevance of this idea for my argument.

There were valid reasons why scholars placed paid work at center stage in South Africa. Frederick Cooper pointed out that "wage-labor capitalism, in most of Africa, takes place on islands in a sea of other sorts of socio-economic relations; in South Africa, wage-labor capitalism pervades the economy" (2002, 194). While such an observation was certainly accurate until the mid-1970s, the importance of paid work has since been on the decline—as, indeed, in many other settings (Ferguson 2015; Parry 2018; Sanchez & Lazar 2019). There are complex reasons, in the South African case, for this steep drop. They include the sudden liberalization of the economy and removal of protectionist barriers, and a process of financialization occurring globally that profoundly reshaped the relationship between society, state, and market, leading to job-less growth and a corresponding decline in labor-intensive industry (Ferguson 2015, 76–83; Hull & James 2012). Nonetheless, the (former) ubiquity of, and reliance on, paid work, as Ferguson and others have acknowledged (Barchiesi 2011), has left in place an assumption that the main route to both a livelihood and citizenship is through employment.

In the UK, similar assumptions are in evidence. The long history of trade union activism over two centuries, entrenching labor rights at the center of social policy, is well known. The Beveridge Report of 1942, alongside proposing a universal social insurance system that included family allowances and the revenue-financed National Health Service, also committed to full employment (Hills 2015). Perhaps more dubious, however, is the prevalence of assumptions about work in recent UK policy and welfare reforms. The post-2010 array of benefits, notably the job seeker's allowance (JSA), continues to place the image of sovereign workers, responsible for their own well-being, at center stage. Although the chances of measuring up to that image are slim, individual research interlocutors often see themselves as between jobs rather than as permanently welfare dependent.

The material on debt presented in this book suggests a kind of third way.

It is certainly the case that a unique focus on wage labor is inadequate to cap-
ture the wageless experiences of many in the twenty-first century (Denning
2010). But veering too far in the opposite direction can be equally problematic. Exploring distributional labor does not simply mean looking at those
who are recipients of welfare or "cash payments"—or at those unsuccessful
in gaining access to these, for whom distributive labor involves "accessing
or making claims on the resources of others" (Ferguson 2019, 90). Instead, it
means exploring the intense efforts of people to negotiate a path in settings
where wage work, once a secure source of livelihood, has ceased to be so. Nor
is the division between the two always clearcut. Instead, in some cases, a person's livelihood may be construed as relying on paid jobs, even where these are
not currently available. Or it may depend in part on intermittent remittances
from a working relative or anticipated—or unexpected—such amounts in the
future. Alternatively, a household head may consider herself to be temporarily
positioned between (sometimes seasonal) jobs. In sum, many of our research
interlocutors were *not* completely wageless (Denning 2010): they defined
themselves by reference to a wage-earning relative—or to a time when they, or
their relatives, did earn a wage and/or were swept up in the large-scale mining
operations of the twentieth century or in its side currents, such as domestic
labor for white or wealthier black people, or to some future time when a wage
might again become a possibility.

Mothers and Grandmothers: South Africa's Wageless?
In the South African case, a person's eligibility for paid work is inflected
by her circumstances in the household and in the life cycle.[3] Many female
grant recipients had been wage earners until a moment when they became
responsible for the care of young children. Some were forced out of work
by the death of a son or daughter whose children needed to be looked after.
Or, as was the case with younger women, a pregnancy made it impossible to
continue their employment. The fact that those most frequently charged with
the task of care—that is, women—have become recipients of payments from
the state is no mere coincidence. The child support grant (CSG) is specifically
designed to enable childcare (Ferguson 2015, 6; Neves et al. 2009), but it never
approximates, nor is it an equivalent for, the wage that that woman previously
earned. The difference between the two, in most cases, is being made up with
loans, as demonstrated by the story of Akhona at the beginning of this chapter.
    Similar stories were told and retold during the research we conducted

around South Africa in 2018 (Figure 1.1). The main focus of the research was on people whose welfare payments (called social grants) were being used as security by a range of lenders who charged excessive interest rates, but our findings also revealed details of those borrowers' work circumstances and histories. While these varied greatly depending on our interlocutors' proximity to urban centers and places of employment, very few cases indicated a completely wageless situation. Rather, recent stints of wage work for private employers were interwoven with current or anticipated contracts for a public works program or with a period of paid employment for an NGO that had recently run out of funds but whose coffers might later be refilled. These were also combined with intermittent (often irregular) payments from wages earned by siblings, children, or other relatives, partly in recognition of, or to compensate for, the childcare they were performing. Such cases certainly

FIGURE 1.1: Map of South Africa showing field sites.
Elsabe Gelderblom, Black Sash.

confirmed that work was casualized and precarious (Parry 2018; Sanchez & Lazar 2019) and that the "proper job" was on the wane (Ferguson & Li 2018). They also pointed to a need for people to perform robust distributive labor in drawing down or securing resources from those who had access to them. But rather than thinking of this as a world without a wage, it is more useful to see it as one in which patchworks of funds (Zaloom & James 2023) are continually being pieced together by those only partially able to earn one.

A number of our interlocutors were grandmothers caring for children in the absence of their parents. Four of them lived in Khutsong, a township adjoining the town of Carletonville, formerly at the heart of the gold mining industry but, since the closure of many mines, a site of rising unemployment. During the mining boom before and up to the mid-1970s, many families moved here from far-flung rural areas: the Eastern Cape and Free State as well as the neighboring countries of Lesotho, Swaziland, and Mozambique. The influx led to a sharp increase in informal housing, and although the post-apartheid government later provided sub-standard RDP (Reconstruction and Development Programme) houses into which these shack-dwellers moved, more people later arrived and took up residence in the shack areas, often paying rent to the former residents.

One interlocutor, Patricia, although currently reliant on state welfare, had worked for many years in neighboring Carletonville—a predominantly white area—as a domestic servant. She was now receiving a pension (OPG—older person's grant) and two foster care grants (FCGs) to care for her son's two children. (Her son and his partner, the children's mother, had both died some years back.) Another, Bokang, likewise reliant on her pension, had suffered a similar loss with the death of her son and daughter-in-law. She had not needed to work until recently, since her son, a teacher, had supported her as well as providing a well-built and well-appointed house where she still lived. That support terminated with his death; not wanting to stay there alone, she fostered an unrelated child, receiving an FCG to help her support her charge. A third woman, Rebecca, was still a wage earner, holding down a job as a domestic servant in Carletonville. She too had a son—he worked as a teaching assistant but contributed nothing to his parents' household. At the same time, she and her husband were both old enough to qualify for pensions (OPGs). Finally, exemplifying the situation of several younger women we met, thirty-four-year-old Letsha, more highly educated than Patricia and Bokang, had earned a reasonable if somewhat irregular living through the commissions for

selling insurance. In a familiar pattern in which paid work provides no ma-
ternity benefits, she was forced to stop work when her baby was born. A single
parent, she was now relying on two child support grants as well as occasional
money gifts from her salaried brother.

We encountered similar stories in the other areas of South Africa where
we did research, although these varied with the context and especially with
the proximity to town. Women's life trajectories had seen them move through
a variety of forms of paid employment and/or self-employment that, by the
time we met them, were no longer available or had temporarily ceased. Alternatively, women caring for children were receiving remittances from menfolk. In both cases, pay from employment was combined with welfare grants
and loans to form a household's income. In areas close to cities with more
diverse economies than Carletonville, such as Pretoria and Cape Town, jobs as
shop assistants (often procured through labor brokers) or working for NGOs
were intermittently available. In Khayelitsha near Cape Town, Lynn Rhadebe
worked first on a flower farm and later as a domestic worker. Similarly, for
Catherine X, the arc of her working life took her from a domestic job to running her own informal daycare center in the township, from whose takings she
was able to pay a regular salary to herself and another care worker, until the
demands of formal registration forced her to close it. In contrast, in settings
much more remote, like Taaiboschgroet near the Zimbabwe border, women
did seasonal work on farms, labored for a few months in a government public
works program or for an NGO, had "piece jobs" doing laundry or fencing,
relied on support from their mothers who did domestic work, got sporadic
contributions from their menfolk who had jobs in security or in the nearby
diamond mine, or drove taxis.

In all these cases the work for which wages were received was, indeed, very
far from resembling the "proper job" of Ferguson and Li's critical account
(2018) or the "standard employment relationship" that Parry rightly says has
waned in recent times (2018). But most of these mothers and grandmothers
were drawing at least some portion of their income from the waged earnings
of a family member or, until recently, had been earners themselves. The work
or distributive labor these women were engaged in, then, was that of piecing
together diverse income sources. A livelihood was being sewn together using
remittances or wages along with other varied sources, including one (or several) grants and many loans.

Part of that labor consisted of making social investments in group support and social relationships, as will be discussed in Chapter 2. Part of it consisted of often quite strenuous efforts to get what was their due from the state. But perhaps the most time-consuming and arduous labor, in this setting where financialization had penetrated so deeply, was that of negotiating with, evading, or challenging lenders to make sure that the terrain of borrowed money would contribute to, rather than drain away, the household's well-being.

Before we examine this aspect, let us turn to the context of the UK, which, although different in a number of important respects, shows a similarly complex relationship among wage work, welfare, and debt in a setting where "proper jobs" have been likewise on the decline.

Mothers, Ill-Health, and Household Management in the UK

During research conducted in the UK in 2015–16, it became evident that work was becoming precarious. At the same time, welfare payments had been reduced and reconfigured because of austerity reforms, and the cost of living was on the rise (James 2022; Kirwan 2018, 2021a). By 2023, following the COVID-19 pandemic, these trends had intensified, as noted in a Citizens Advice report.[4] My fieldwork in some London debt advice offices gives anecdotal insights into the relationship between work and welfare. A varied range of people, many of them working part-time or in the gig economy, were seeking counsel on how best to balance their budgets (James 2022, 66). While those I met were a mix of male and female advisees, a parallel study conducted around the same time notes that "women, being both responsible for more complex household finances and more likely to be chased for jointly held debts following relationship breakdown, are more likely to be seeking debt advice" (Kirwan 2021a, 161). And, at that time, those in the most precarious and unstable jobs were more likely to be "Black, Asian and Minority Ethnic," as official UK terminology then had it.[5] Many were recent migrants from Africa, the Caribbean, or Latin America. Indebtedness, then, had a particularly gendered and ethnic character.

Beyond these features, a noteworthy aspect of the work experience of those I encountered was the way their work histories had been interrupted by ill-health, whether mental or physical. As was the case in South Africa, those holding down precarious or part-time work, or who ran their own businesses, did not qualify for employer-provided illness benefits to tide them over, although there was some state provision, albeit dwindling and subject to rigorous eligibility checks, of disability allowance. Of the men I met, several were self-employed (e.g., as electricians), others worked full- or part-time for security firms on so-called zero-hours contracts, or as cab drivers for Uber or Addison Lee. Others were pensioners, or students who worked part-time while studying. Of the women, one had run a hair and beauty business while others had been employed in domestic service or as cleaners. Many, having previously earned some or all the family's income through wage work, had since quit paid employment. They did so mostly because of illness, depression, and/or other problems with mental health.

As in the South African case, these periods of employment—some expired, others ongoing—were interwoven with reliance on state benefits. And as in South Africa, it was those who, with childcare obligations, were out of work who were entitled to payments specific to their circumstances—child benefits or child tax credits—alongside others to be outlined below. Although there were, in our study as in Kirwan's, some "whose income was drawn from long-term sickness and disability benefits," there were others who "described moving between minimum-wage employment (cleaning and care work in the case of the women) interspersed with periods of living on . . . benefits" (Kirwan 2021a, 161).

Although these benefits are considerably more varied and substantial than they are in the South African case, they, too, never make up for the wages that their recipients previously earned. And thus, as in the South African case, the difference between the two is often compensated for with loans. Here there is evidence of a marked change: Sam Kirwan points out that "the model of debt advice, predicated upon reducing expenditure and maximising income, and thus constructing a balanced budget that can be used both to negotiate with creditors and to assist the client in avoiding further debt, 'just doesn't fit anymore'" (2021a, 170). In other words, "incomes and expenditures simply do not match, often forcing people to borrow in order to pay rent and other crucial expenses" (James 2022, 60).

Getting Benefits, Distributing Debts, Countering Repayments

Distributive labor has, then, undoubtedly become increasingly important as women, in particular, make efforts to patch together a living from diverse sources. This patchworking—in an era where the boundaries between (public) welfare and (private) debtfare are increasingly blurred (Montgomerie 2016, 418)—requires ingenuity as householders seek access to resources that support their reproduction and their future plans for greater stability, well-being, and even wealth (Zaloom & James 2023). If by "labor" we mean strenuous activity and if by "work" we imply "effort in negotiating socioeconomic relations" (Bandelj 2020, 258), then the endeavors undertaken by people in these low-income settings certainly qualified. The endeavors required were both dogged and relentless. But they were, in many cases, less concerned with *securing* a loan than *combating* its automated repayment once it had been secured: what I call "counter-deductions" (James 2017).

Here I try to simplify, by providing schemas of, two parallel and contrasting kinds of assemblages—one public, the other provided through private finance—that predominate in the two settings. One is the UK's system of welfare benefits, while the other is South Africa's arrangement, perhaps equally systemic (if not intentionally so), of borrowing opportunities. The division between the two is not wholly clearcut. In the British case, for example, recent austerity cuts to central government and local authority funding have reduced these publicly provided sources of livelihood, meaning that those in need are pushed increasingly towards providers of loans in the private sphere (Soederberg 2014). In the South African one, in contrast, publicly funded grants have been made widely available but are so small as to make it almost inevitable that recipients end up using them as collateral for loans borrowed from private providers. These loans are used, in many instances, to make up for the lack of forms of public provision *other* than cash payments: for healthcare, educational equipment, and the like. They have also often been used, in this country where the HIV/AIDS pandemic took so many lives, to help pay funeral expenses in the event of a relative's untimely death.

In the UK, in addition to the two benefits provided to givers of childcare mentioned above, a range of further payments were available from a variety of sources (Table 1.1). The resulting landscape—until welfare reform was phased in to replace it with the allegedly simpler system of universal credit—was a complex one that mostly required expert advice to navigate. Some, such as JSA (job seeker's allowance, known historically and colloquially as the "dole") and ESA (employment support allowance, to supplement the incomes of disabled people) were provided centrally by the DWP (Department of Work and Pensions). Some, like working tax credits, were also provided centrally but by a different department: the tax office, known as HMRC (Her Majesty's Revenue and Customs). Others, like housing benefits, were paid by local authorities or councils (Forbess & James 2014; James 2022, 69–70).[6] Following the

2010 Coalition (later Conservative) government's austerity-oriented welfare reforms, this jigsaw-like assemblage was being replaced, in the interests of simplicity, by a single welfare payment dubbed universal credit, but this much-decried transformation had still not been fully accomplished by 2024. In part, as observed by critics of this reform, the delay was itself due to the fact that each household had particular needs and particular circumstances—a fact ignored by the designers of the "universal" solution.

The rigorous means testing of such benefits, and the pursuit of those who were seen to have misrepresented their earnings or their circumstances, made for a far stricter welfare regime than South Africa's. In combination, these could add up to an income that sometimes, but with decreasing frequency, was able to provision a household adequately. Its inadequacy was particularly evident in the costly circumstances of London. Especially for these women with childcare obligations, considerable work—perhaps distributive labor— was required to activate or claim these payments or challenge the authorities when these were discontinued. In many cases, this was done with the assistance of advisers, as Chapter 4 will demonstrate.

In South Africa, in contrast, the range of available benefits is simpler and more restricted, and all are provided in the form of cash transfers by a single department: DSD (Department of Social Development) through its agency SASSA. SASSA, in turn, has outsourced the task of delivering the payments. As outlined above, this was initially done by Net1/CPS until the contract was withdrawn in 2018; then it was given to the publicly run SAPO (South African

TABLE 1.1: Benefits in the UK (before introduction of UC)

Benefit	Agency
Job seeker's allowance: JSA ("dole")	DWP
Employment support allowance: ESA	DWP
Personal independence payment: PIP (formerly DLA)	DWP
Child benefit: CB	HMRC
Child tax credit: CTC	HMRC
Working tax credit: WTC	HMRC
Housing benefit: HB	Local authority/Council
Council tax support	Local authority/Council

Post Office). Over the intervening years, however, SAPO has been in decline and has proved inadequate to the task, and many grant pay points have been decommissioned. At the time of writing, welfare beneficiaries thus had a reduced set of options for drawing their cash. Those with bank accounts were able to do so from an ATM, but these are in short supply, especially in rural areas. Another alternative is to access payments via a retailer, but this meant recipients are usually obliged to spend part of the grant at that shop.

This combination of a simpler set of benefits with a reduced means to access them has led, in turn, to a reliance on loans. If we turn back to the case of domestic cleaner Akhona at the start of this chapter, we will remember that her child support grants (CSGs) and monthly wage were supplemented by regular loans from Moneyline. Repayments for these loans were being automatically deducted by the lender, which was a subsidiary of the company distributing the grants. In South Africa, in other words, the income landscape depicted in Table 1.2, showing the situation as it existed in 2020, is not one of public benefits (though these underpin it) but one of private loans.

Table 1.2 attempts to make sense of the practices by which grant recipients get loans transferred to them by lenders, and then repay these. Although it follows a series of gradations from seemingly formal to increasingly informal practices, from left to right, the forms of borrowing and lending it portrays defy a simple categorization along these lines (Hart 2015), since many face-to-face cash transactions rely on, or are facilitated by, the original transfer of grants to recipients via high-tech debit orders using sophisticated banking infrastructure. Interest rates vary widely, as do the ways in which these are communicated to borrowers. The registered lenders on the left-hand side of the table publish their rates on preprinted forms with carbon copies given to borrowers, and generally comply with the stipulations of the National Credit Act (NCA), although high-interest rates are often obscured by calling these "initiation" or "service fees" (Gregory 2012). The *mashonisas* (loan sharks)[7] on the right-hand side of the table, in contrast, mostly charge higher rates of interest, comply with no legal stipulations, and often fail to record repayments or inform borrowers of their remaining debts, or do so only by using ATM "mini statement" printouts or recording loans in exercise books.

Lenders in the left-hand column, such as Moneyline and Finbond, rely on sophisticated financial arrangements like the the EFT/debit order system and the functionality of Net1's EasyPay Everywhere or EPE card. Moneyline is a registered financial services provider and a subsidiary of Net1; Finbond

TABLE 1.2: Lenders in South Africa

Lending Context	Lenders					
Transfer/Repayment	EFT/Debit Order	Cash/Debit Order	Cash/Cash	Mashonisa (small)	Mashonisa (medium)	Mashonisa (large)
Examples of lenders (to social grant recipients)	National/Corporate EPE/Moneyline (facilitated by CPS/Net1), Finbond	Regional ABC, Top-Up, Mashabalala	Regional/Local Payday/Chinese lenders (e.g., Wen, Zhang)			
Social connection	None	Little to none	None	Kin, neighbors	Stokvels, slightly larger, more distant from borrower	Largest, most socially distant
Terms of the loan	3- to 6-month loans, about 5% interest per month (excluding fees)	3- to 6-month loans; about 30–60% interest per month	1-month loans, given in cash; about 30–60% interest	30% interest monthly, does not retain borrower card, negotiable terms and timeframe	30–50% interest, may retain card but not PIN, less negotiable terms and timeframe	50–100% interest, retains card and PIN, little negotiation
Characteristics of lending system	High-tech, biometric-verification, formal printed contracts	Hybrid system: combines formal banking or payment system with cash disbursement of the loan, written or verbal contracts	Personalized and relational: relies on ATM banking/cards to claim repayment, but uses informal handwritten or verbal contracts or ATM statements			

is a mutual bank partially owned by Net1. Both are large firms with multiple branches nationwide. Because banking the unbanked had initially been made possible through the contract awarded to Net1/CPS that afforded it a kind of "lock-in" (Breckenridge 2019; Torkelson 2020), this enabled debit order–based lending and automatic debit order deductions for social grant recipients, even following the termination of its contract to distribute the grants themselves. Other microlenders with debit order facilities—and even those without—were able to piggyback on these Net1 innovations. The second column includes lenders that grant loans in cash and collect repayments using debit orders on borrowers' bank accounts: enterprises offering cash and payday loans that may have several branches but are regionally based and much smaller than the large financial services companies or mutual banks. Their loans are repaid by debit order on a bank account. The lenders in the third column both lend to borrowers and collect loan repayments in cash. The size of their businesses, the nature of their relationship with borrowers, and the interest rates charged vary, but they are generally described as *mashonisas*. Those most distant from their borrowers in both spatial and relationship terms charge interest that, at 50–100 percent per month, is the highest recorded (James et al. 2020, 2022).

This table may seem unduly complex. Indeed its intricacy is such that expert help and advice may seem indispensable in order to claw back what is due. The situation it represents also seems to beg for some form of regulation (James et al. 2020). What mainly concerns me here, however, is the way that individual householders view the distributional labor they perform to combine and stitch together, from this array of public and private sources, a patchwork livelihood.

"I Advise Myself"

Something has changed since Ferguson published his 2015 book *Give a Man a Fish*. In that book he challenges the "productivist," work-centered approach taken by academics and policymakers and urges that we see the furnishing of cash transfers—and welfare payments more broadly—in a more positive light: as representing people's rightful share of some broader wealth held in common. He maintains that this might promise a new kind of politics, one based not on proletarian struggles and Marxist-style worker solidarity, but on participation in that wider collectivity or common weal. "The giving out of grants," he maintains, seems to transcend, or pledge a more effective redistribution of wealth than the "militant political demands for state appropriation of land

and industry" (2015, 168) that South Africa's transition originally promised. He aims to bring these latter, more strident, kinds of demands "into relation" with those that cash payments might enable.

He likely could not have foreseen the extractivism, described by some as looting, that occurred when the distribution of those grants by the private company Net1/CPS, to whom the contract was awarded, was paired with the granting of loans by its subsidiary Moneyline, using regular payments into beneficiaries' bank accounts as security. Nor could he have anticipated the cascading of other loan possibilities (see Table 1.2) that piggybacked on those EFT-based payments. These developments evoked much critical discussion in the media and in the academy, as well as widespread protest and several court cases.[8] It was as a result of this outcry that the contract was eventually withdrawn from the private company concerned. The voices raised in criticism were indeed, as Ferguson intuited, protesting the removal of an entitlement—the share that each citizen felt was her prerogative. What fewer of these accounts acknowledged was that the money being borrowed by welfare recipients was, itself, one component of that same share. Hence, while the idea took hold that lenders with their often unreasonably high interest rates were threatening to reduce a family's assemblage of income, it was equally true that being unable to access loans of any kind would be similarly injurious.

It was in compiling both grants and loans, alongside wages and remittances, into an overall portfolio—but one with separate components—that householders were endeavoring to make real their claims to what they felt was their due. The two vignettes at the start of this chapter show how women were itemizing separate elements of a budget, setting aside money from these divergent sources to achieve different ends. One used her loans specifically for transport, while the second was paying particular expenses with her two credit cards. In a similar vein, Ariel Wilkis's work in low-income Buenos Aires neighborhoods shows how a householder parcels her finances up into separate conceptual bundles or "pieces of money" (with "borrowed money" featuring merely as one of these), occasionally converting one into the other strategically, in a manner informed by moral calculation, political necessity, or the need for social continuity (2017).

Anthropologist Fiona Ross (2010) documents similar tactics in a shack area of Cape Town. She shows how the management of a series of income sources, including debts, often necessitates making decisions that are subject to scrutiny by relatives and neighbors, which might need to be reassessed and altered. The experience of a woman called Sandra involved patching together not only different types of monetary value but also divergent senses of time. Owing money both for her son's school fees and to complete her installments on a set of storage shelves that she paid a "lay-bye" to secure (if she failed to honor the agreement by a certain date, she would forfeit both the unit and the payments already made), she combined careful deliberation with trust in providence. She used the money set aside for school fees to pay off the cupboard, presuming later to be able to rely on a relative's help for the fees or "pay them off over the year." The choice was between education (for which others might be pressured into paying) or respectability and social propriety (the costs of which would have to be borne by the household). The choice paid off, since a well-wisher gave money for the school fees, while owning the cupboard enhanced her status (see Guérin 2014; James 2020, 204; Ross 2010, 131).

Although an outside analyst or advocate of financial literacy, like policymakers in both the settings here considered, are rightly concerned about the long-term sustainability of patchwork approaches like these, the examples that follow suggest that householders are often more canny than we may recognize, since the avoidance of repayment sometimes enables them to take advantage of the possibilities of the wage, grant, or loan assemblage in unexpected ways. As will emerge over the following chapters, those who are living more remotely (or further below the radar) are sometimes those least likely to benefit from formalized channels of advice. They must, then, do as Patricia of Khutsong told us she does. Asked whether she had been able to seek counsel about her debt problems, she said "I advise myself."

Opportunities and Self-Help Strategies

In research among Dalit villagers in South India, Isabelle Guérin and Santosh Kumar found that monetary debt "opens up opportunities and possibilities," including for relationships that encompass economic as well as other elements (2020, 230). But these opportunities are not handed to householders on a plate. Earlier, Guérin, together with fellow authors Solène Morvant-Roux and Magdalena Villarreal (2013), coined the term "juggling" to describe the savvy expertise that is required to take advantage of them. In South Africa, I noted that township dwellers in Tembisa, near Johannesburg, were skillfully negotiating their finances, "alternately using their bank accounts and letting them become dormant, alternately repaying or avoiding their obligations to retailers, sometimes taking out more expensive loans to pay off cheaper ones, and borrowing from informal lenders or becoming lenders in their turn—sometimes all at once" (James 2015, 171). Loans make new prospects available but have knock-on effects that require intense effort to manage and negotiate.

This observation holds true in both South African and British settings, but I focus here on the former. In the cases from our 2018–19 research with Black Sash, some women had borrowed money for specific and necessary purposes. The use of credit is described in the literature as "smoothing" normal consumption (Ardington et al. 2004, 607; James et al. 2020, 22). Amounts were not subsumed into an undifferentiated mixture of income sources, but rather envisaged as part of a budgeting exercise. Transport was often mentioned as a major expense for which women had borrowed. The legacy of apartheid has meant that country dwellers often live far away from schools, healthcare facilities, shops, and the like. Seasonal changes and calendar events required recurrent and regular borrowing in order to buy summer and winter uniforms as children outgrew last year's clothes. These loans, being predictable, could be taken out from EFT-based lenders like Moneyline, with their relatively lower interest rates.

However, there were also those who had lived without borrowing until an unforeseen event had necessitated a large expenditure. Credit, in addition to "smoothing consumption," is often glossed in the literature as "coping with shocks" (Ardington et al. 2004, 607; James et al. 2020, 22) or dealing with crises beyond the normal run of events. Key among these, in a number of cases, was the death, and subsequent funeral, of a family member: an event much commoner in South Africa, as a result of the HIV/AIDS pandemic, than it used to be—and later COVID-19. Although almost all householders had taken out funeral insurance and/or joined savings clubs in anticipation of such an eventuality, the expenses involved in burial and its accompanying ritual were such that these never provided enough (see James et al. n.d.; Thomson & Posel 2002).[9]

Whether routine, semi-expected, or coming out of left field, household needs that led to taking out loans were thus approached by some, at least, with shrewdness. They knew what could be borrowed from which lender, when, and for which purposes. In the small coastal town of Port St Johns (see Figure 1.1), David Neves found that, in the face of the "complexity of the decision-making about borrowing, including the constant cycle of repayment and borrowing," householders "readily enumerated a range of reasons for preferring *mashonisas* or simultaneously borrowing from both" (James et al. n.d., 139).

One reason was that banks, in accordance with official regulations aimed at curbing "reckless lending," will lend only to those who can furnish three months' pay slips or bank statements as proof of a regular income (James et al. n.d., 139).[10] The alternative is to borrow from Moneyline, using one's welfare grant as security and repaying at interest rates lower than those charged by *mashonisas*. Sometimes money borrowed for longer-term investments is repurposed to help with an emergency. In one rare case, an EFT-based loan taken out for home improvements (by someone who had earned the trust of the lender through a history of conscientious repayments) did end up being diverted to funeral costs.[11]However, EFT-based lenders will not normally lend money for such emergencies. Given these constraints, urgent needs for cash often lead a person to approach a *mashonisa,* who provides a necessary (and approachable), if expensive, alternative.

Indeed, by some, these informal lenders are routinely favored over EFT-based ones. Yandisa, a resident of Port St Johns, needed funds to rebuild her house. Asked why she preferred always to borrow from a particular *mashonisa,* she explained that this lender does not pressure her to repay and is "respectful." Borrowing from the registered, and hence legally endorsed, EFT-based lenders "would require transport, and seeking them out." She "anticipates she will borrow again" in order to finish the rebuilding. "There are always demands on the money with three grandsons—so it always gets spent. It is therefore easier to borrow," she remarked. The "continual cycle of borrowing and repayment" could therefore be seen, said Neves of his discussion with Yandisa, as "a money management technique" (James et al. n.d., 104–105, 157). Similar cases have been observed elsewhere in South Africa, in which individuals try to ensure they have a minimum of cash on hand, lest it be drawn upon inordinately by needy relatives. For example, it is common to pay a deposit as a lay-bye or as a down payment on an item of furniture, which then obliges one to keep up monthly repayments. Such obligations can then counter, or be used to politely back out of, requests from kin for financial support. Even "putting aside money regularly in order to honor one's obligations to particular kinsmen" can "stave off further demands from each intended recipient beyond what these instalments stipulate" (James 2021, 48).

Overall, despite the disadvantages they face, women with access to social grants (and to the loans for which the latter have served as security) have devised novel ways of patching funds together, taking advantage of various options to negotiate across the terrain of diverse wage sources, welfare payments, and lenders as they seek to grapple with the differentiated temporalities of the credit cycle while also confronting unforeseen events. Rhythms of shortage, set by grant payments and shortages rather than the seasonal agricultural cycles that structured temporalities for their grandparents, must be offset by longer-term plans. The experience of lack that typically occurs in the middle of the welfare payment cycle (i.e., midmonth), or in the middle of the six-month repayment period offered by EFT/debit order lenders like Moneyline, predispose grant recipients to extra borrowing, often—because they have few alternatives—from the most extractive of lenders. But, as Chapter 2 shows, they often use the loans to pay into social savings schemes that count as longer-term investments (see James et al. 2022, 69–70).

So much for the possibilities offered by loans, the essentials of livelihood and sociality for which they pay, and the effort that must be expended in establishing when and where to borrow. However, what of the claim made by debt activists, legal and human rights advocates, and others, that the high interest rates and automated repayments ultimately result in hardship, that they reduce the already pitifully small amounts afforded by welfare payments?

Female householders were often all too aware of this repayment effect, while also recognizing that the original intent behind the provision of welfare was a redistributive one. Reiterating that intention but bemoaning its decline, Alice Kumi in Delft maintained that "Mandela . . . was a good person. Mandela gave us these grants for the children. He was a good president. I don't know who's the president now." Patricia of Khutsong said, "It's good that the government helps us—in other countries they don't get this. . . . But the money is not enough. . . . I could do something else with that money they take from me." Said Kate of Taaiboschgroet, referring to the extortionate interest rates being charged by loan sharks, "It is painful, because we are getting grants but these do not reach the household—they are just received by the *mashonisas*" (James et al. n.d., 50, 127, 167).

In response, many devised self-help tactics. Catherine in Khayelitsha "practised a strategy of paying a nominal R100 monthly" and "pretends to be someone else" when the phone rings. She asserted "that it is wrong to 'lead my children into poverty' by making larger payments, arguing instead it was the shops and others (corporate creditors) that ought to 'suffer'" (James et al. 2020, 51). Others hid from informal lenders or, seeking safety in numbers, chased them away with the help of groups of friends and neighbors (James et al. 2020, 52). In Khutsong, Patricia's approach, along with belt-tightening, evidenced determination to avoid lenders altogether. "I advise myself," she said, and avoids "going deeper and deeper" by restricting consumption. But this involves deprivation: "I told my kids 'this month you'll stay hungry because there's no money.' I haven't gone back there, till now" (James et al. 2020, 129).

Showing unusual bureaucratic savviness was Phumza in Uitenhage. Instead of engaging in evasive action, she showed an awareness of citizen/consumer rights. Having borrowed from a cash lender, she used her monthly statement from SASSA, the welfare agency, to demonstrate to that lender that they had made undue deductions. She thereafter succeeded in getting a letter testifying that she had repaid in full, which enabled her to resist further excessive demands from that lender (James et al. n.d., 191).

Overall, these women were balancing income sources such as intermittent wage-based remittances against the welfare payments that had become available in the wake of the democratic transition and were seizing the opportunities offered by the credit that various lenders were offering. They also felt, in the spirit of what Ferguson calls the "fair share" (2015), that welfare payments were what was due to them. The distributive labor they performed, then, involved a balancing act in which they resisted undue demands from kinsmen and also countered the automated deductions that were taken by lenders in repayment.

"Giving with One Hand and Taking Away with the Other"

The three-way relationship among sources of income discussed in this chapter—wage labor, welfare payments, and loans—has acquired a very particular character in the UK. The "welfare myth of them and us" (Hills 2015), proposing an unwarranted dichotomy between those who work and those who might never gain paid employment, is widely subscribed to in that society where the tabloid press regularly, and infamously, pronounces on the prevalence of "welfare scroungers." That myth obscures the fact, central to my argument in this book, that many beneficiaries are simultaneously wage earners. John Hills's account of income, taxation, and redistribution shows how the original idea of the welfare state was one of a world in which risks were shared over the life cycle and where "you could not neatly divide the population into those who paid and those who received" (see Fraser & Gordon 1994, 323; Hills 2015, 4).

Subsequent to the founding of that welfare state, a succession of governments has tinkered with the ways in which benefits are reckoned and balanced against earnings. The complex arrangements whereby disparate state agencies make diverse payments, noted above (see Table 1.1), were mostly designed with progressive aims in mind. Working tax credit and other benefits administered by HMRC, for example, were introduced in 2003 by the New Labour government under Chancellor (later Prime Minister) Gordon Brown, to encourage people to work, and to respond to the increasing flexibility of working patterns (Hills 2015, 2; Millar & Whiteford 2020). They were also aimed at serving a moderate but important redistributive function in favor of the poorest households (Hills 2015, 226). The 2010–2015 government, a coalition between the Conservatives and Liberal Democrats, aimed to change all this. Again in the name of responding to changing working patterns as well as consigning undue complexity to the past, their Welfare Reform Act of 2012 proposed to replace these "legacy benefits" with a new system, universal credit, administered centrally by the DWP (see James & Kirwan 2019, 672–676; Kirwan 2021b; Millar & Whiteford 2020).[12]

Underlying these reforms, however—and likely their true motivation—was a new ideology of austerity that saw the earlier, comparatively generous and wide-ranging provision of welfare payments—as well as the advice required to access these—progressively withdrawn. It is partly to this turnabout that some of the peculiarities of the UK's current benefit system can be traced. In this, too, lies the reason for drawing a direct comparison between South Africa's complex credit landscape and the UK's equally complex topography of benefits (see Tables 1.1 and 1.2).

In the two years leading up to 2016, debt advisers noted that their clients, previously troubled by debts to conventional commercial lenders (credit and store card companies and payday lenders) were presently more concerned about being in arrears with rent, electricity bills, or council tax payments. These are known as "priority debts" because the consequences of non-repayment are more serious than those involving a commercial creditor. While the latter can result in the repossession of movable assets like televisions or electrical equipment, the former can result in eviction. The crucial point to note is that many of these, especially for those partly or wholly dependent on benefits, are debts owed to the state (James 2020, 69; James & Kirwan 2019, 2021b; Kirwan 2018; Schwartz & Spooner 2021; Spooner 2021). Thus, where welfare recipients in South Africa were borrowing from (and owing repayments to) an array of private lenders, those in debt in the UK were more significantly in arrears to public ones: whether the local authority, the taxman, or the central welfare department. Many of these debts had resulted, in the first place, from being paid too much by one or other of these authorities. The means through which these overpayments were being recouped was via debit orders, deductions from future welfare payments, or demands for repayment through other means. As discussed in more detail in Chapter 5, one key reason for the demand to give back overpaid benefits—that is, for being in debt to the state—was the combining of work and welfare as sources of income.

The way this procedure works is as follows. Under the welfare reforms noted above, recipients are obliged to keep authorities up to date on changing circumstances that affect household income—especially work for wages (see Koch 2015). An "overpayment" demand is triggered when authorities discover that a person has brought in more earnings than reported, and hence received undue benefit payments. In one case, "a woman decided against taking part-time work; benefits were providing only just enough to survive on, but they were predictable, and a wavering income would upset these delicate arrangements." Similar demands for reporting are required, and commensurate readjustments made, by the revenue office, HMRC (James 2022a, 71).

In sum, the sudden suspension, or reduction, or demand for repayment of one benefit can, in effect, be a penalty for not fulfilling the conditionalities attached to another (Patrick 2017, 43–44). The process of trying to switch from depending on benefits to work wages, as encouraged (and stipulated) under welfare reform, means that such benefits are continually readjusted because the number of hours worked, especially on zero-hours contracts, is inconstant. It is because the weekly wage earned by those on such contracts can vary so widely that these part-time workers are more liable than their exclusively welfare-dependent counterparts to having their benefits overpaid. Among the most recently publicized and widely condemned of this kind of phenomenon, to be discussed in Chapter 5, has been DWP's demand that people doing part-time care for elderly or sick relatives, and receiving carers' benefits, repay those benefits because of earning "too much" through any other paid work.[13]

It is with respect to these automated deductions to which beneficiaries are subjected that SA's (private) and the UK's (public) systems most closely resemble each other. In addition to such deductions, however, some UK welfare recipients find themselves faced with large bills for amounts discovered retrospectively to be owed because of overpaid benefits. These bills result from several processes. One is the outsourcing of the burden of reporting their circumstances to benefit recipients, rather than checking their eligibility in advance.

A second is calculating payments based on the previous year's end-of-year total income, which often results in errors. Finally, there are official "errors," usually stemming from the authorities' failure to act on the information that *has been* provided. In recognition of these, the system was tweaked in 2008: "If you fulfil all your responsibilities," it was announced, "we won't ask you to pay back all of the overpayment arising from our failure." The DWP itself estimated that £3.5 billion was "overpaid" in 2012–13, because of combined "fraud" and errors by administrators or claimants, with two thirds of this because of (officials') "error" rather than (recipients') "fraud" (Hills 2015, 263).

Since the topic of overpayments is taken up in more detail in Chapter 5, I here use just one example to briefly illustrate the interplay between wages and the receipt of benefits. The story also gives a foretaste—elaborated in Chapter 4—of how essential a role is played by empathetic advisers in the UK. Yusuf, an adviser at the North London Muslim Community Centre, based in Stoke Newington, told me the story of one of his clients. Yusuf occupied a previously full-time post, funding for which had been cut under the new austerity regime. Following the cuts, he was funded under a partnership coordinated by an NGO called Social Action for Health (SAfH) for fourteen hours a week, an amount topped off by a further six hours following a decision by the board of the Community Centre. Yusuf offered advice to all and sundry—advice much appreciated because of his knowledge of the rapidly changing welfare benefits regime and the personal links he had cultivated with specific officers in the local authority. But in practice it was often non-English speakers who approached him, in view of his linguistic abilities in Urdu and Gujarati. Yusuf told me about a client who received an overpayment demand. The client

> got a letter—he had been overpaid £16,000 for Housing Benefit and Council Tax Benefit. They sent a breakdown. I phoned Hackney Council. [They said] "we have checked with HMRC—he has two jobs, one for a security firm." "How did you get this?" "We cross-referenced with HMRC" . . . . [They said] "we are using good systems." I said, "no, there is a mistake." They argued. [I said], "I guarantee I will get the information." They said "we have to do what it says on the screen." So we phoned HMRC and got his income details, and a letter. It looked like [he was working for] two companies, but . . . one had changed its name. We gave in the information. Thankfully, the Housing Benefit one was updated. But they didn't recalculate the Council Tax Benefit. They should have reassessed both. Later we wrote another letter, and this time it worked.[14]

The stories of how adviser and client sought to pursue these and other similar challenges is certainly a story of counter-deductions in the face of repayment demands. But since it speaks less of self-help (as in the South African cases mentioned above) than of a struggle mediated through the help of an adviser, I pursue it, with other similar stories, later in the book. I include it here, however, because it illustrates several themes pertinent to the present chapter. First, it shows the intricate entanglement between diverse sources of income—especially work and welfare—in the UK setting, as in the South African one. Second, it illustrates the considerable efforts required by householders in order to piece together these constituent elements to amass the funds that might constitute a livelihood and the intrinsic value and necessity of such assemblies to their well-being. Third, if we add in the third element of our discussion here—loans—it shows the even more strenuous exertions undertaken to defend whatever funds are available against the imperative to repay: to private lenders in the South African case and to public welfare agencies in the UK one. In both these settings, distributive labor is not merely a matter of cultivating dependencies, social relations, and informal loyalties in the absence of wages. It also involves work to sustain a delicate and necessary balance between those wages and other income sources.

Conclusion

The material presented here seems to paint a bleak picture. In South Africa, where welfare has only recently been rolled out, social protection has taken the form of small cash transfers. These are inadequate, making it necessary for recipients to borrow, and driving them into the arms of sometimes unscrupulous lenders that use both high-tech and more personal means to secure repayment. While lenders seem immune to the risk of non-repayment because automated systems mostly make this unlikely, borrowers—reluctant to let their monies feather the nests of moneylenders—endure undue stress in fighting to retain access to what they see as their due.

In the UK, a related kind of struggle is underway. Although welfare provision—including healthcare, education, and the like—was more comprehensively introduced in the post-war period, austerity regimes are now cutting it back, together with the advice necessary to gain access to it. Where welfare states may once have promised citizens access to the basics of education, healthcare, and even housing, state retrenchment has devolved responsibility for these necessities onto individuals (Brown 2015; Langley 2009) or families (Cooper 2014; Zaloom 2019). This was done, in part, notes Wendy Brown, to eliminate the docility of the welfare claimant: to transform the person waiting passively in the "dole queue" into a self-motivated and independent citizen (2015, 84, 110). This aim, she argues, is almost impossible to achieve because, when considered together with claimants' other obligations, the additional requirements and conditionalities have taken a toll on the capacity of individuals to maintain caring obligations and other practices of householding (Brown 2015, 103–104).

Seen from one perspective, then, the material presented here may seem to exemplify a situation in which corporations and governments alike have imprinted priorities on their citizens and subjects, customers and clients, rendering them as "risk-bearing subjects" (Christophers et al. 2017) through various forms of financialization and by turning welfare, in different ways, into debtfare. But the cases presented in this chapter give some insight into how high-tech abstractions of financialization, whether operated by private companies or governments, interplay with relational encounters among borrowers, lenders, and advisers in local settings, as well as showing how debts are interwoven with the other sources from which households gain their income. The distributional labor involved requires the ability to convert between different registers that belie "any clear distinction between public and private provision of necessities" (Zaloom & James 2023). Later chapters will further demonstrate how low-income South Africans strive to conserve the payments they get from the state and guard them against "looting" by private lenders, while UK welfare beneficiaries attempt to keep whatever benefits they feel they are due, conserving these in the face of insistent demands for payback from the government.

TWO

Redistribution or Debt?
Rechanneling Financial Flows

REDRESS FOR HARMS, COMPENSATION FOR INJUSTICE—these are common themes in today's world (see, for example, the demands at the UN's Conference of the Parties in 2022 by smaller, less developed countries for climate change reparations). Redistribution can encompass a wide variety of meanings, ranging from these high-level and high-profile examples such as the redistribution of land in the wake of political change, right through to much more everyday, mundane ones, and from formal taxation through to less organized arrangements. This chapter addresses how the two levels intersect.

Redistribution is no longer (if it ever was) just a matter for the state (whether at national or local level). In settings where financialization is accompanied by increased informalization, it can involve the market as much as the state, and it can involve funds moving upwards as well as downwards. The extent to which some form of compensation or redress is accomplished varies depending on the perspective of participants—a point that might sound self-evident but whose complexity I will try to illustrate by showing that notions of fair practice are contested and context-specific.

The form of redistribution I discuss here is one that depends on, is mediated by, and can even be undermined by, processes of financialization. Although welfare payments have in some cases been caused to dwindle as creditors demand repayment, I nonetheless challenge approaches that imply a uniformly one-way, top-down intrusion of market logics into intimate family and social relations. In this perspective, financialization disciplines families to understand their lives in its terms and to act in ways that reproduce the formalized demands of financial contracts. Anthropological examinations of finance and its effects on other aspects of social life, in this framework, reproduce binary thinking about the stark separation of commodified and non-commodified relationships. The chapter aims to complicate, and contest, such an approach (see James & Zaloom 2023). Let me start with a case study: the story of a woman enmeshed in family and neighborhood obligations but whose grant payments (and borrowing) have caught her up in wider structures.

From Peter to Pay Paul?

Mpho lives in a remote settlement, Taaiboschgroet, in the far north of South Africa, in Limpopo province, not far from the Zimbabwean border (see Figure 1.1 in Chapter 1). She lives with her partner, who is twenty years older than she is and has never been employed, and their three children, all of whom are in school. The household subsists partly on welfare payments from the government, consisting of three child support grants totaling R1,260 monthly (£64.26; $99.50) plus the earnings from her work (a temporary, unstable job) in an NGO that offers home-based care to sick people and that yields R3,500 (£178.50; $278) monthly. There are various expenditures and outgoings. Crucially for my story, these include repayment on three loans: one (involving a so-called Green Card and done via electronic funds transfer or EFT—hence more apparently formal in character) to Moneyline, and two others to *mashonisas*. The *mashonisa* loans also involve a level of formality but with some personal intervention, in that one of them (at least) confiscates the Green Card (Figure 2.1) and uses it to extract repayments from the ATM. She borrows R1,000 (£51; $79) from Moneyline every six months, and before taking out the next loan she will have repaid R1,320 (264 percent per annum, or 22 percent per month: an amount allowed by the regulator). These loans she sees as covering recurrent and seasonally specific expenditures such as school clothes and daily necessities. The two loans from *mashonisas* amount to about R3,000 (£153; $237), with an interest rate set, illegally, at 50 percent per month (Table 2.1). In practice, though, repayments are often negotiated and sporadic, and they can endure over unspecified periods of time. These less regular loans are for unforeseen expenses, such as traveling by minibus taxi to take her child

FIGURE 2.1: Grant recipient with EPE's Green Card.
Erna Curry, Black Sash.

TABLE 2.1: Mpho's income sources and debt repayments

	Work	Welfare	Debt	Repayment
Income source	NGO (intermittent)	Three child support grants	Two loans	
Amount	R3500	R1260	R1000— EPE, six monthly R1500— *mashonisa,* ad hoc R1500— *mashonisa,* ad hoc	R1320— six monthly R2250— monthly R2250— monthly

to the doctor. Her borrowing also helps to fund outgoings deemed socially necessary—such as contributions to neighborhood associations and savings clubs aimed at providing for funerals (James et al. 2020, 49; James et al. 2023).

Understanding this case requires some wider context, as exposed during the research I and my fellow researchers did with human rights NGO Black Sash, which was aimed at working towards redress and greater fairness in combating unregulated reckless lending. First, there are high levels of financialization, whose onset and steep rise more or less coincided with the moment of democratization in 1994. The new government, acutely aware of the need for welfare provision—one aspect of redistribution, enacted by the state with funds from the treasury—delivered social grants to more than 17 million people. By 2024, the number had reached over 26 million.[1] This post-democracy inclusion of black people as beneficiaries of a welfare state that previously catered largely to whites is seen by Jeremy Seekings and Nicoli Nattrass as signaling a "distributional regime" (2005, 314; see Breckenridge 2014, 164–195). Expanding on that characterization, I and my co-author Elizabeth Hull have spoken of this as a setting where "neoliberal means interweave with and facilitate redistributive ends" (Hull & James 2012).

But it is also one where the opposite is true: where redistributive resources are diverted to enable market profits and fill the coffers of large financial corporations. The delivery of these social grants was initially outsourced to a multinational company, Cash Paymaster Services (CPS) with its UEPS (Universal Electronic Payment Systems) Technologies, known as Net1. The Green Cards it issued (see Figure 2.1) enabled EFTs. Taking advantage of its monopolistic position and the "lock-in" this facilitated (Breckenridge 2019), it made use of the grants as security or collateral. These in turn facilitated the offering of high-interest loans to grant recipients, using "pre-agreement statements" via Net1's subsidiary Moneyline. It was through these arrangements that Mpho, as noted above, was recurrently borrowing R1,000 every six months. The automatic repayment of these loans via debit order, and the less automated repayment of others, comprise an economy with an unhealthy reliance on "deductions" (James 2017b).

Following the initial efflorescence of such lending, however, "counter-deductions" began to gather steam. Numerous authors documented—and deplored—the way in which this system of grants-cum-loans was functioning to deplete the meager resources of welfare beneficiaries (Donovan 2015; Neves 2018; Torkelson 2020; Vally 2016). Supported by Black Sash, widespread protest erupted around the country in a "Hands Off Our Grants" campaign (Figure 2.2). Despite some reforms, however, the use of grants as loan security continued. Our research with Black Sash aimed—in the absence of other reliable data—to establish the continuing extent of this practice in some far-flung rural areas (James et al. 2020). As we discovered, it remained widespread. Here was a rather different aspect of redistribution. In what amounted to "trickle up" rather than "trickle down," state funds were serving to enrich a variety of private lenders to whom borrowers were making automated repayments at high interest (on loans that were, strictly speaking, not "unsecured" because their repayment was guaranteed by the state).

As noted earlier, we devised a diagram (see Table 1.2 in Chapter 1) in an attempt to replace the binary counterposing of economic formality with its supposed opposite: informality. It illustrates the matrix of lending relationships in which someone like Mpho was enmeshed. The system of EFTs enabled by the Green Card, outlined on the left, not only enabled the automated repayment of the debts owed to Net1's subsidiary Moneyline; it also established the basis of an effortless flow of further repayments to other lenders, in the middle and on the right-hand side of the diagram. "Financial inclusion" into elec-

FIGURE 2.2: "Hands Off Our Grants" protestors.
Black Sash

tronic file transfer arrangements was thus setting the scene—and establishing the platform—for all these subsidiary forms of borrowing and repayment that depended on it.

Mpho's story speaks to many themes and conundrums addressed below, but for the moment let me crystallize just one of these by posing a question in overly binary terms. The question echoes anthropology's age-old concern with structure versus agency, but with an added dimension. Is Mpho—at the sharp end of the numerous displacements, disturbances, and disadvantages that are the long-term heritage of apartheid—now the unwilling and uninformed victim of its most recent manifestation: namely an unregulated system in which the market is flooded with credit, in which usurious interest rates are charged with impunity, and in which little financial education or debt advice is available? Should we see her bank account as a space for untrammeled "looting"?

Or, mindful of the imperative to "invest" money in social relationships rather than "eat" (that is, "waste") it (James et al. 2023), and using her access to welfare payments (and to the loans for which these serve as collateral) as best she can, is she finding the best way available to her of navigating the complex credit terrain? Are her borrowings evidence of innovative ways of practicing household budgeting as well as investing in broader solidarities, by juggling between the diverse lenders and differentiated temporalities of the credit landscape and its complex cycles (Guérin 2014)? Could the attitude of Mpho and her counterparts, like that of the low-income householders in Buenos Aires studied by Ariel Wilkis, be summed up as "we don't have money, but we do have debt" (Wilkis 2017)? This view might suggest that, while offering credit at extortionate rates offends all liberal notions of justice and properly policed rights, having access to it at any cost—and involving personalized relationships in gaining that access but also using it to boost or invest in these—is crucial for those who need it.

I focus here on two moments or levels in a story of redistribution: the local level where Mpho and others like her are either stymied by, or find ways of navigating their way through, the confusing array of financial devices, and a higher level where activists, advisers, and mediators, further attempting to "counter" this seemingly unsustainable system of deductions, interact both with market actors and with officials from government departments. The role of some of the former is noted in Chapter 3. In respect to the latter, the two government departments (Table 2.2) have their own priorities and accompanying

TABLE 2.2: Diverging doctrines of government departments: DSD and DTIC

Department of Social Development (DSD)	Department of Trade, Industry, and Competition (DTIC)
Mpho is a victim of an unregulated credit system: her bank account is for "looting"	Mpho is navigating a complex credit landscape to enable "social investment"
Protection/paternalism	Right to trade and constitutional right to property
Amendments to Social Assistance Act (2016)	Section 10 of the constitution
Must protect children's temporary grants from deductions: grants must not be "transferred, ceded, pledged, or in any other way encumbered or disposed of"	Laws that curb a beneficiary's ability to enter into a contract limit the right to dignity, from which freedom of contract springs

ideologies and are mostly at odds with each other. Put in simple terms, one favors an approach that enables paternalistic protection (which would curb Mpho's borrowing practices) and the other embodies the economic freedom promised by the country's constitution (which would allow them to continue). But, in their search for possible remedies to what some see as an egregious undermining of the redistributive impulse that underpinned the original roll-out of welfare payments, the two aim to move towards a compromise if not a consensus.

These two approaches, taken by two government departments, align roughly with the two ways of seeing Mpho's situation, as stated above. Having posed them in overly binary terms, I now explore what possibilities exist for activities at these different levels, and attitudes towards these, to converge, or whether they remain irreconcilable.

Welfare, Work, or Distributive Labor

As noted in the Introduction, it is the state that has both acted on behalf of capitalists and the market, while also intervening to ensure that workers are compensated for those disadvantages for which capitalists and the market have been responsible (Elster 1991, 273; Fraser 2014; Therborn 2012, 587). Work is often scarce or precarious, although it has not disappeared altogether. Bear in mind that, although Mpho *did* have a job, it was an unstable one. Other people we encountered worked at daily-paid seasonal labor or government public work schemes, but few of these led to union activity or collective bargaining and few involved payment into the state treasury. While redistribution—the payment of cash transfers or social grants—*was* being accomplished using funds from the tax base, the government department responsible had outsourced their disbursement to the private company Net1, whose collection of debt repayments was causing grant recipients' monthly stipends to dwindle.

In the face of these threats to the size and regularity of welfare payments, one source Mpho and others like her were using—a form that predated the onset of these grants—was that noted above: neighborhood associations and savings clubs aimed at providing for funerals (James et al. 2020, 2023). Known locally as a *stokvel* (from the English "stock fair")—*umcalelo* (in IsiXhosa) or *lehodisana* (in SeSotho)—this type of club, dubbed a "financial mutual" in the academic literature and typically taking the form of a rotating savings and credit association (ROSCA), has been a feature of rapidly urbanizing societies worldwide, from China and Indonesia (Geertz 1962) to sub-Saharan Africa (Ardener 1964, 2010; Bähre 2007; Krige 2014; Kuper & Kaplan 1944; Rodima-Taylor 2014). Members contribute standard amounts at regular intervals throughout a cycle (usually a year). They then take it in turns at monthly meetings, or when urgent needs arise, receiving the accumulated amount in cash and using it for expenditures normally beyond their reach.

Although these clubs are often seen as traditional, they are not in fact rooted in ancient custom (Shipton 2007). In black South African communities, they emerged, instead, in tandem with oscillating labor migration and urbanization (Bähre 2007; Kuper and Kaplan 1944). Often they responded to the need to repatriate the bodies of deceased migrants and help with other burial costs (Delius 1996; see also Thomson & Posel 2002). Women's clubs, emerging as female migration became commonplace, provided a means to save earnings as well as support and solidarity (James 2015; Mager & Mulaudzi 2012). They are nowadays often seen as quintessentially female, being associated with investment in social relations and care for the household, whereas men are often said (by women) to be more inclined towards "eating" (that is, wasting) money (James et al. 2022). Women such as Mpho, attempting to get by on state welfare payments and the uncertain returns from precarious jobs and typically charged with the responsibility for householding and husbandry, are using these clubs to invest rather than "eat" money. Their membership of *stokvels* serves as a contribution, and sign of commitment, to solidaristic social relationships.

These and other similar kinds of relational strategies have been commented on by James Ferguson (2012, 2015) and Tania Murray Li (Ferguson & Li 2018). In post-liberation South Africa, says Ferguson, the sovereign subject whose well-being is predicated on labor is being eclipsed by the non-sovereign one with a life centered on relational dependencies. Rather than trying to squeeze more and more people into an ever-smaller category of the employed, a new politics of distribution—involving cash transfers or basic income grants—would, he claims, enable a world of well-being based on dependency, accompanied by political demands for the "fair share."[4] Further, Ferguson and Li (2018) discuss "non-productivist" scenarios that, they argue, should be thought of as "emergent realities" with their own characteristics: as much "social and affective" as material, as much based on "gender and generation" as on simple wages, and as much based on social relations and informal loyalties as on contracts.

These observations chime with others that point to the unavailability of work and to some that document the avoidance of wage work even where it is to be had (Dawson 2022; Denning 2010). Ferguson speaks of "distributive labor" to evoke the efforts put into building relationships and social ties by those, devoid of wage work, who seek to cultivate and maintain connections (2015; Ferguson & Li 2018, 12). The term conjures up images of (inter)dependence, in contrast to the autonomy of the individual worker earning a wage sufficient for the well-being of her family. Such observations raise questions about how, in the relative scarcity of work (and especially of organized labor), provisioning and welfare will be afforded. How might this alter or moderate the claims outlined earlier: that redistribution is a process set in motion by non-market initiatives to counteract the iniquities produced by the market—especially by exploitative labor relations?

Ferguson and Li provide some answers to such questions. They mention the existence of new social protection programs dispensing cash transfers, in countries (such as South Africa) that "we are not used to thinking of as welfare states" (2018, 11). They also mention "various strategies for tapping into streams of income controlled by others," such as "dependence on patrons or kin." Such relationships cannot be taken for granted; rather, cultivating and maintaining them involves "distributive labor" (2018, 51). By such a reckoning, the redistribution of income thus involves both states and less formal social relations—precisely as the case of Mpho illustrates. It echoes anthropological insights about how all humans are enmeshed in endless and intricate webs of relationality.

My ethnography, however, points to conclusions somewhat at variance with these authors' claims. Firstly, where they note the virtual disappearance of the "proper job" and with it the sovereign subject whose well-being is predicated on labor, and where they criticize social policy wonks and academics alike for continuing to emphasize wage labor, it is precisely the *existence* of work (albeit low-paid and precarious work) that complicates the picture of the dependent subject entirely reliant on distributional labor. Low-paid work in the UK, for example, causes problems to those advising clients who are trying to square the triangle of wages, debts, and welfare benefits, as I show in Chapter 5. Secondly, Ferguson's somewhat utopian predictions of the opportunities for collective mobilization presented by South Africa's social grants system did not encompass what was coming down the line—that is, the use of these government payouts to poor people as a sort of loan security by large financial companies using them to press grant recipients into borrowing and repaying. Since the onset of those processes, much distributional work has, in fact, needed to be devoted to securing or clawing back what *is* a rightful share, in the face of the financialized actors that both provide resources and, simultaneously, threaten to confiscate them through future repayments.

Savings Clubs, Distributive Labor, and Loan Sharks

Countering the implicitly positive-sounding attributes of "distributive labor," there is a more extractive aspect to savings clubs, in particular. If by "redistribution" we mean the spreading out of income to level inequalities arising in the market, we are defining it by reference to its intended advantageous outcome, seen largely as beneficial to the broader social fabric. But if we include processes, often informal ones, through which resources belonging to one person or set of people are taken and reallocated to others, not necessarily for the good of all, we might include a variety of other arrangements. The salient question here is "distribute to whom?"

We find ourselves coming up against scenarios that are uncomfortably ambiguous, in part because they are viewed in different ways depending on the point of view of the observer. Take the example of moneylending or loansharking—one element of the story of Mpho with which this chapter began. This is the ubiquitous practice, now widespread in South African township areas, in which money is lent—especially, though not only—to recipients of welfare payments. As noted in the case of Mpho, a *mashonisa*, once having issued a loan, uses such future payments as security, keeping the borrower's ATM card (or Green Card) until the end of the month when she can withdraw the loan plus interest—typically 50 percent per month—from the borrower's account. This practice is criticized by organizations such as the Black Sash, because it seems to condemn borrowers to an unending cycle of debt as well as unduly enriching those lucky enough to be able to accumulate enough money to start such a lending operation. The practice is also denounced because it serves to benefit lenders by giving them unearned income: they are, in effect, leeching off the state and using the welfare recipient as an unwitting conduit—or "bridge" as one person put it—to channel that income. Loansharking here ensures that one form of redistribution (given out by the state to combat unemployment, poverty, and malnutrition) is turned around and becomes something very different.

Such condemnatory perspectives, however, somewhat miss the point. The ambiguity of the situation is seen when one digs deeper and explores the ways this informal practice intersects with others, particularly by looking at the forms of "social calculus" involved (Bear 2015). First, borrowers often view these lenders as doing them a favor when no alternative source of credit— "fairer" or readily available in emergencies—exists. Instead of blaming lenders, they point to the fact that moneylenders are "doing a service," that they are the friends rather than mere "clients" of such lenders (Krige 2011, 146), and that they, the borrowers, are to blame for their neediness or inability to husband their resources. Second, as I have previously noted, borrowers cannot easily be separated from lenders (James 2015, 144). The *mashonisas* are often members of savings clubs who have been able to gather up a lump sum only because of belonging to such a club, with the rules (or "constitution") often specifying that members are obliged to lend out that lump sum with interest and will themselves be liable for the payment if their "clients" fail to pay back the loans (with interest added). Women like Mpho who juggle diverse sources of income—wages, grants, and debts—may find themselves borrowing from savings club members. (At the same time, they too belong to savings clubs and may end up borrowing from *mashonisas*, as Mpho was doing, in order to keep up their club contributions.)

A further case, that of Patricia from Khutsong in Gauteng (see Figure 1.1 in

Chapter 1), is an example of a *stokvel* acting as *mashonisa*, but at lower interest rates. Patricia, herself previously a member of a *stokvel* that had recently disbanded, was advised by her fellow members to approach a woman who belonged to another such savings club that was known to offer loans. She asked to borrow R3,000. The normal practice would have been to have her repay R3,900 the following month (at 30 percent interest). Instead she negotiated, asking whether she could stretch the payment over three months—R1,300 each month—but without further interest. "I told her that I don't want to suffer." They agreed verbally on these terms and conditions. Instead of keeping Patricia's Green Card, this lender came to fetch the card at the end of each month. "She trusts me, she knows where I live." She withdrew what was owed to her, then gave Patricia a mini statement, so Patricia could see what had been taken. "That one was very good, she didn't cheat you." This lender had her own cash-flow problems: on this occasion she only had enough cash to give Patricia R1,200 of the total R3,000 in the first instance, and gave her the rest later on. The lender was far from wealthy, but her *stokvel* membership gave her access, barely, to the necessary funds (James et al. 2020, 43; James et al. 2022, 65).

Overall, these entangled systems of lending and repayment can obscure, or complicate, any simple notions about who is compensating whom for the unfortunate twists and turns of market-driven economy, and about whether such compensations originate with, or depend upon, state, market, or civil society.

What Is "Economic" and What Isn't?

To discuss the ways in which a woman like Mpho juggles her income—whether she needs paternalistic protection or requires the freedom to act in a way that seems to serve her own best interests—we need to go over some ground concerning what economic rationality really is. In Malinowski's *Argonauts of the Western Pacific*, he highlights how the myth of an "imaginary, primitive man" in "current economic text books" must be exploded: one "prompted in all his actions by a rationalistic conception of self-interest." "The primitive Trobriander," he says, is

> prompted by motives of a highly complex, social and traditional nature, and towards aims which are certainly not directed towards the satisfaction of present wants, or to the direct achievement of utilitarian purposes. (1922, 60)

Soon after the birth of modern fieldwork-based anthropology in the 1920s, the utilitarian-centered version of economics—emphasizing rational choice and the maximizing individual—began to predominate, while the one that more holistically incorporated ritual action, belief, and social relations received less emphasis. As the century wore on, various scholars, many drawing on Polanyi's influential work—among them Keith Hart, Chris Hann, Stephen Gudeman, and David Graeber—sought to revive that suppressed tradition by showing how what economists were now calling "externalities" were in fact central to what they were now calling the "economic." Mauss's essay on *The Gift* (2016) as interpreted by some, was less about how primitive economies had been arranged (in contrast to commodified ones) and more about how, transcending both "primitive" and "modern" economic systems, a "non-contractual element in the contract" has existed and been central to exchange in all societies (Hann & Hart 2011; Hart 2007).

Not always included in those who celebrate this tradition of scholarship is the work of Clifford Geertz. As noted in the Introduction, his early work in Indonesia, *Peddlers and Princes* (1968), highlights some of these "externalities" or "non-contractual elements."[2] It pointed to schemas of value, ethics, relational mores, forms of social embeddedness, and the like, which were foundational to the work of economic transaction and its accompanying calculations. In his later, and recently republished, short monograph on the *sūq* in Sefrou, Morocco (Geertz 2023), he demonstrated another social/relational modality through which seemingly economic transactions are filtered. Highlighting the important roles of specific participants, Geertz showed how the holders of specific roles perform actions that, together, serve to integrate the various components of the bazaar economy. As intermediaries positioned between various groups, these individuals helped to "create" the bazaar by judiciously disseminating information and, in the process, by balancing the needs of knowledgeable participants against those of less knowledgeable ones. For each, it is of crucial importance to sort through a thicket of information, combining the available evidence to try to get clues about "how things stand" at any given moment. Certain aspects of the bazaar economy facilitate this and others obscure it.

Thus, while the bazaar *seems* to approximate the "nearest thing . . . to the purely competitive market of neoclassical economics . . . where profit-making sellers confront utility-maximizing buyers" (Geertz 2023, 79–80), communication in and of itself, and by its very nature, is imperfect and makes any objective view impossible. Geertz shows how words and concepts relating to ethical life—such as trust, judgment, obligation—are invoked, activated, and strategically manipulated by the various participants in the transactions involved. All of them bear the responsibility to decide about whom, what, and how much to believe (and conversely in whom, what, and how much to confide), not least because each player is striving to uphold his reputation in the small terrain where he operates. "Truths" are relational, but also personalized.[3]

I find this suggestive in focusing in on, and understanding, the motivations of Mpho and others like her. That's all very well, you might say, but the Moroccan *sūq* was a relatively small-scale institution with relatively clearly assigned roles and expectations, often mapped out along ethnic lines between protagonists like large-scale Jewish merchants, smaller-scale Jewish peddlers, and Berber pastoralists. In any case, all of these were upended when the French took over Morocco as a protectorate in 1915. Would it not be anachronistic to read modern-day welfare grant recipients and owers of money—as well as those who advise them and attempt to ameliorate their predicaments—in similar terms, not least because it underestimates the absolute power of large, high-tech, financialized corporations such as Net1?

The context is certainly different, but Geertz's insistence on bringing diverse relational logics and perspectives into the understanding of economy is nonetheless useful. Let me turn back to my ethnography. Our work on the distribution of welfare in South Africa, the way it is received and used by its beneficiaries, and the efforts made to combat the steep rise in their indebtedness in recent times reveals similar situations to those he describes. In these, relevant information is only partially available to each party in the encounter. I maintain that—using Weberian "methodological individualism"—one can view matters from the standpoint of each of these parties, rather than glossing them and insisting that they be embedded in (and seen as automatically subordinate to) an extractive or exploitative structure and insisting that local-level borrowers must be encouraged to counter that exploitative dimension.

Seeing things through this prism enables a new and rather different perspective from that laid out in the schema devised as part of the Black Sash research project. Wearing the hat of left-liberal analysts, we were trying to understand the phenomenon of unregulated or semi-regulated reckless lending throughout South Africa. We mapped this with a diagram (see Table 1.2 in Chapter 1) that suggested an overall extractive logic, with the EFT system on the left-hand side structuring and enabling a set of subsidiary lending arrangements and repayments that expand from it towards the right-hand side. Financial inclusion into EFT arrangements sets the scene—and establishes the platform—for all these other, dependent forms of borrowing. As we saw it, "preferential access" to a huge market was "handed to the corporate lender CPS . . . in 2012"; lending by *mashonisas* and by "cash lenders" depends on "the highly technological and biometrically facilitated banking platform enabled by Net1/CPS" (James et al. 2020, 13–14).[4]

Seen, instead, in the way Geertz depicted the *sūq*, these partly-intersecting but partly distinct worlds of lending establish a complex set of relationalities: a kind of matrix within which various actors' perspectives partly match each other but at times diverge. If one takes the case of Mpho outlined above (as well as others, such as those outlined in Chapter 4, in which advice is offered to borrowers), one might say that the various participants in the borrowing/ debt encounter (and in the advice or activist-intervention encounter, in those cases where such a thing exists) have unequal access to information—not necessarily, or not only, because any one protagonist is cynically withholding vital knowledge from others, but also because the social life circumstances of each are distinct and it is only in the moment of interaction that they are juxtaposed or brought into the same frame. Mpho's case demonstrates an intentional *denial* of information. She seems unwilling to compute how much she owes to the two *mashonisas* in total: "if you could remember that amount of money, you would get a heart attack," she told me. Mpho was able to use her own particular scale of temporality to juggle grants and loans in the interests of her family, while also using loans from *mashonisas* to keep up her subscription to funeral clubs, thus enabling her to retain her status in the neighborhood. This was the "social calculus" (Bear 2015) she made—the particular form of distributive labor she undertook (Ferguson 2015). In such moments where different actors are brought into temporary juxtaposition, alternately mediated by high-tech processes and personalized relations with local lenders, redistributive encounters are created, in a manner similar to what happened in the *sūq*.

Advisers, activists, and policymakers, depending on their positionality, alternately celebrate decisions such as Mpho's as embodying "freedom of choice" and view them as requiring paternalistic intervention. Both have a point, and the two sides of the argument have been robustly argued.[5]

Beneficiaries, Brokers, Bureaucrats, Advisers

If the work of Mauss and others points us towards the "non-contractual element in the contract," part of that non-contractual element lies in the hands
of the brokers, bureaucrats, and agents whose importance I outlined in the
Introduction. I noted there that South Africa has far fewer advisers, and that
their activities are funded more sporadically, than in the UK. Part of the
work with Black Sash aimed at remedying this lack. It involved Stellenbosch
University Law Clinic, revising and updating a handbook on debt and credit
that was originally published at the start of South Africa's "debt epidemic"
(2021). This we used in a series of workshops for community paralegals and
their clients, still ongoing at the time of writing.[6] In the absence of a wider
penetration of any debt advice into rural areas like the one where Mpho lives,
it was during these training sessions that key questions arose about issues of
accessing social grants, their use to repay loans, and the like. "This is when we
find out what 'clients' actually want," as one of the trainers put it.

At workshops held during 2022, advisers and clients alike were indeed
keen to find out more about their rights. They wanted to know whether there
were debt relief mechanisms they might be able to access, what to look out for
when entering an agreement or signing a contract, what counts as fair, what to
do when getting a threatening letter, how to cancel a credit agreement once it
has been paid off, and how to handle "historical debt" such as that owed to the
government company issuing student loans. Issues were also raised relating
to consumer rights—for example, about low-quality goods being sold to them
by local informal shops (the only source of food for kilometers). There were
also questions about *stokvels* and other savings clubs, which of their activities
are legal and which are not, how to draw up a constitution for such a club,
and related issues. Interestingly, and illustrating the point that borrowers
and lenders cannot be easily separated, just as "the economic" is difficult to
mark off from "the non-economic," those seeking help and advice at these
workshops have included not only borrower clients but also informal lenders
(*mashonisas*) interested in registering with the National Credit Regulator but
unsure about how to do so.[7]

It is here that I return to the question of how policy deliberations play into
my study of redistribution. If encounters involving financial systems are often
facilitated by intermediaries or brokers, in what way does (or can) an anthropologist, collaborating with interlocutors in the human rights fraternity, serve in

such a role—and can (and ought) they strive to provide "full information" to all participants about these matters? Or will the nature of that information necessarily remain partial and personalized, as in the *sūq* of Geertz's account? There are, at first glance, some obvious answers to the last question. No one is all-seeing, and there is, of course, no unmediated platform on which one can stand to know the "real truth." Nevertheless, there seem to be small ways in which groups of collaborators bent on achieving some positive impact can bridge particular knowledge gaps and sew together some insights into the situation.

Let us look again at Table 2.2, which shows how the two views of Mpho's situation mapped onto the concerns of the government departments charged with matters of welfare and those concerning the regulation of credit, respectively. Welfare issues fall under the Department of Social Development (DSD), while credit issues are the concern of the National Credit Regulator, which in turn is governed by the (recently renamed) Department of Trade, Industry, and Competition (DTIC). Our work on the survey that resulted in the 2020 report (James et al. 2020) highlighted a fundamental clash between two forms of legislation—one falling under DSD, the other under DTIC. DSD wanted to earmark its grants and prevent them from being "alienated" (as occurs when they are used as security for debt repayments), while DTIC paid attention to the need for individual economic freedom: a neoliberal-sounding value that celebrates free choice and individual enterprise and repudiates the paternalistic protections that have sometimes prevailed in pre-democratic South Africa.

The work of brokers/mediators (including human rights NGOs, charities, and anthropologists) in the "redistributive encounter" (see Long 2001) has involved seeking a path that tacks *between* these extremes, rather than subscribing completely to one or the other. In our work with Black Sash, this has involved a set of slow but persistent efforts by our collaborative team—researchers together with Black Sash officers—inviting representatives from these different government departments to meetings. If at times they are too busy to attend, they are then re-invited to subsequent discussions and stakeholder workshops. In these, agendas for action often seem to advance only at a snail's pace, and yet once a small gain is made it seems to be relatively stable. The difficulties in moving forward are often caused precisely by the fact that agents from seemingly irreconcilable worlds are having to be brought together. But those normally isolated in their separate silos have begun to listen to other points of view.

A key finding of our report for Black Sash, as noted above, was that the legislation emerging from these two government departments was incompatible. At a series of meetings, the question of harmonizing that legislation was explored. Might it be possible to bridge the gap between two seemingly irreconcilable approaches? Discussions centered, in particular, on child support grants (the welfare payment that people like Mpho were receiving). Following the uproar over the role of the private company, Net1/CPS, in extending loans and extracting repayments, an act was passed by DSD—the SASSA Act—to attempt to curb the practice of deducting repayments automatically from grants. The act stipulated that a deduction of a maximum of 10 percent may be taken, with the specific purpose of paying for funeral cost, but the grant itself may not "be ceded or transferred." In order to enable only these deductions and disallow any others, the solution that had been arrived at was to pursue further digitalized automation. DSD employed a private company, Q-Link, to oversee the process.

The sticking point, however, concerned the transfer of the grant into the recipient's own bank account. At the moment of transfer, the money ceased to be subject to the rule stipulating the maximum deduction of 10 percent. Effectively, the grant from that time onwards was no longer within the (paternalistic) jurisdictional remit of DSD, becoming subject, instead, to the free-market orientation of DTIC. Commensurately with DTIC's preferred approach, once transferred into the person's own bank account, the grant money was deemed to be that person's own property. The key issue here concerned the right of any citizen to take control of, and "own," their own finances. Circumscribing the use of these funds, which were being paid to guardians of children for their care, was seen as being unduly paternalistic, denying these guardians the right to property that had been newly affirmed by the constitution during the democratic transition. The DTIC, and the National Credit Regulator (NCR) that fell under its control, were thus neither willing nor able to insist on protecting the remainder of the money (90 percent) that was supposed to remain with the grantee after the maximum 10 percent had been deducted. Or, if it had conceded the necessity of doing so in the case of the child support grants, it seemed to be leaving other grants susceptible to looting through deductions.

One participant from Black Sash queried, during a meeting:

> having noted the gap in the two legislations, are there any prospects of DSD and DTIC addressing this gap? The fact is that grannies are finding themselves in debt.... Regarding the SASSA Act, we were told "once we have paid the grant, it is outside SASSA's concern." ... Now we have dealt with the children's grants, it seems to be OK for any other grant to be used as collateral.

Another observed "it appears that the shift to automation is inevitable" but wondered whether there would be any initiatives to provide grant recipients with access to these high-tech systems. At the time of writing, these discussions were ongoing.

One might observe that the protective or paternalistic aspect embodies a commitment to full transparency. It lays bare—if seen in purely economic terms—the profiteering that goes on (and makes evident the full extent of interest paid), as well as proposing ultimately to make it impossible for people like Mpho to take out loans that would rely on their child support grants as security for repayment. The freedom to trade and constitutional rights-based aspect, on the other hand, seems to endorse the continuation of the system as it presently stands, in which the invisibility of profiteering is maintained but people like Mpho would be able to carry on taking out loans (albeit often unaffordable ones), making it possible for them to invest in social obligations such as those represented by funeral clubs. Taken to extremes, my application of Geertz's insights into the *sūq* might suggest that people like her would prefer to be left in the dark since that would enable them to continue borrowing, in order to fund the kinds of social investments to which rational calculus is ill-suited.

Assuming, however, that vulnerable consumers *would* benefit from access to a fuller array of information, a second set of collaborative efforts by our team have included exploring how debt advice might be provided and funded, possibly by exacting a levy on financial companies (a system that has been formally adopted in the UK). With my colleagues, we co-authored a comparative paper (James et al. 2021) exploring how similar arrangements work in the UK, Brazil, and Croatia, which was discussed—and debated fiercely—at an online meeting (and which I explore further in Chapter 4). In contrast, and resembling an earlier arrangement in the UK, South Africa has a more voluntary arrangement: the Office of the Financial Ombud (NFOSA), to which financial companies belong (and pay membership) on a voluntary basis. Getting further with a proposal for a mandatory levy, and a properly funded advice sector, would likely involve bringing yet another department— the national treasury—into discussions.

Conclusion

For South Africans with an unstable status as wage workers—and for those whose prospects of employment are small to nonexistent—official redistribution from the treasury, via an array of welfare payments or social grants—is routinely supplemented by borrowing. The loans are made by large financial companies that have been enlisted by the state to provide regular welfare payments, but the companies have also used these payments, in turn, as security to ensure those loans are automatically repaid with interest. Recipients may use the money they borrow both to pay for healthcare or transport, but also to invest in social well-being (especially through savings clubs) rather than its purely economic equivalent. It has been my argument here that, for these people, both debt itself and attempts to ameliorate its most egregious effects can be analyzed as forms of redistribution.

However, this should not be viewed monolithically. We might tentatively suggest a differentiation between how those with adequate or rising incomes deriving from employment by the state or the market, and those without steady wages who have fewer resources, depend on the market, the state, and the NGO sector. Anthropologist Erik Bähre has shown how, for middle-class people with salaried or other forms of income, making insurance payments into a central pot, with the expectation of later receiving pay-outs in cases of hardship, is feasible, and has the knock-on effect of enabling them to dodge excessive ties of relationality: a situation he dubs the "ironies of solidarity" (2011, 2020). I have shown elsewhere how, for teachers and others who *do* have stable earnings, their investment in savings clubs and in formal insurance schemes on behalf of relatives can enable them to do a moderate amount of "social" investment. But it can also serve to "cut the network" (Strathern 1996), preventing their own earnings from leaching away and thus foreclosing on *too much* "social" (James 2015). For those on low or no wages, like Mpho, the equivalent engagement with big finance is less via insurance than via small, high-interest loans, which (in contrast) are then used, outside of formal arrangements, to cement and consolidate their "social/solidarity" dependence.

We can here reconsider the high-level discussions between government departments and NGOs about credit reform. The proposal implemented by DSD moves towards intensifying financial formality, suggesting greater involvement with the sector represented on the left-hand side of the diagram in Table 1.2 in Chapter 1. Such a move would leave people like Mpho, "once the money has moved into [her] own bank account," to negotiate the lending matrix as they are best able; this strategy is commensurate with the DTIC approach that gives individuals the right to manage their own assets in an unregulated manner.

By exploring a particular case in some detail, this chapter has unpacked how—and why—debt is used and managed. Borrowing from Peter to pay Paul can serve as one kind of distributive labor. In what might seem like "wilful blindness" (Bovensiepen & Pelkmans 2020), the debtor uses a calculation that is as much social as economic, finding ways to underplay the extent of her debt to one creditor while paying her arrears to another. Her right to do so reflects—all the way up the scale to the policy level—her choice, buttressed by free market ideology; the proposal that she needs safeguarding echoes with an alternative discourse, shared by activists and welfare authorities alike: that of protection. Here we find exemplified South Africa's "distributional regime" (Seekings & Nattrass 2005, 314).

We return to these themes of freedom versus protection in the next chapter, still set in South Africa, but with a more explicit focus on how debt and wage labor intersect. The chapter explores a foundational court case that took place some ten years earlier than the events recounted here. The court case laid bare a practice in which large commercial lenders, via the use of "garnishee orders," used the regularity of the *wage* as loan security (Roth 2004, 78). It presaged—and established the logic (perhaps even the explicit foundations) for—the use of regular *welfare* payments for the same purpose. During the case, those seeking to protect wage earners (even from their own propensity to borrow) found themselves centering their attention on the question: "how much [of the wage] is enough?" The lenders, claiming in contrast that free market choice was central to a robust economy (and even to the well-being of their debtors), emerge as having had acquisitive motives, as driven by the aim of diverting that wage away from its earner and into their own pockets.

THREE

How Much Is Enough?
Battling Wage Deductions in the Courts

THIS CHAPTER EXPLORES two of the elements in my triad of livelihood sources: workers' wages and debt. Although, as already noted, the setting is one in which unemployment has soared and paid work has dwindled (Ferguson 2015; Ferguson & Li 2108), the people in the low-paid sector described here—farm workers, cleaners, supermarket shelf-packers, and the like—*do* have paid employment, albeit of a precarious and casualized character.

This story is one that could only have emerged at a specific moment, although the seeds were sown in earlier times. A streamlined system had, for decades, enabled commercial lenders in South Africa to make deductions from these wages before they were received by those who earned them. But the practice intensified during the 1990s. South Africa's moment of democratization saw a boom in the offering of high-interest loans to those previously mostly excluded from being able to secure credit, but now keen to move up in the world. This coincided with a period of "jobless growth" in which there was liberalization of the economy, its opening up to foreign markets, the undercutting of local employment opportunities, and a consequent turn—in the absence of investment in manufacturing and production—to the expansion of the finance sector (Hull & James 2012).

What followed was a steep rise in indebtedness, which in turn generated a heated response by those concerned with protecting uninformed and vulnerable borrowers (James 2017). As part of this, there was discussion about whether such borrowers would at some point be in a position to take charge of their own finances, wages, and accounts rather than requiring continued protection. As I have noted in an earlier publication, there seemed to be a need

> to reform what was, in effect, a system of "external judicial control" . . . one biased in favor of creditors . . . to yield one in which individuals, with the help of appropriate advice and guidance, eventually took control themselves, in the way normally expected of a modern, responsible citizen. (James 2015, 77)[1]

I showed that "much effort was expended by state and nonstate actors to implement systems of financial education and 'wellness' to persuade *borrowers* to do this. Making *lenders* accept such responsibility might require more stringent means" (James 2015, 77). I also offered some insight into the evolution of this tradition of "external judicial control." South Africa's history is one in which workers' wages have long been viewed as something for others to manage. In the case of the nineteenth-century traders who offered young African men advances on their wages, the intention was to get them into debt and then enlist them as migrant laborers. Colonial officials, with a paternalism that has echoes elsewhere in my story, regulated this practice, replacing it with a system of deferring paying wages until workers had returned home, in order to curb them from spending in allegedly immoderate ways and thus diverting the funds from "legitimate uses," including the payment of taxes. Neither labor recruiters nor government administrators regarded such wages as belonging properly to the earners themselves (James 2015, 97–98).

The case study on which I focus here is drawn from court files and interviews that depict a protracted, and fierce, set of legal battles.[2] The struggle was over the legitimacy of subjecting workers' wages to automatic subtractions, and whether such deductions were (in)valid, (il)legal, harmful or beneficial (and to whom)—and (in the longer term) "constitutional." Such subtractions have long been a site of contestation, with various protagonists seeking (on behalf of wage earners) to move against these automatic subtractions and activate "counter-deductions" (James 2017). The use of a war-like metaphor is appropriate: as will be seen, the activities of those on either side of this conflict could be characterized as a sort of arms race.

The EAO Battle

At the center of this case was a controversy over the widespread use in South Africa of garnishee or emoluments attachment orders (EAOs). In this system of debt collection, when a debtor defaults, the lender presents that debtor's employer with a court order. Once such an order has been signed by the employer, and countersigned by the employee herself, it is issued by a magistrate's court against the wage of the debtor, entitling the creditor to take a portion of the debtor's monthly pay before the employee receives it, with the creditor bearing a 5 percent charge (James 2015, 61–64, 74; James & Rajak 2014, 455–456).

This system of debt collection is not unique. It is also used in the US, in the UK, and elsewhere (Carruthers 2022, 8). But abuse of the system, in these settings, has led to increasingly robust and intense regulation (Stephan van der Merwe 2021, 153–205). In contrast, in the South African case, whatever regulation existed was, by the early to mid-2000s, being widely ignored. Shortly after credit arrangements were liberalized in the 1990s and a virtual epidemic of indebtedness followed (James 2015, 5), it became evident to lawyers and paralegals, often those working in university law clinics such as those in Pretoria and Stellenbosch, that garnishee orders were causing wage earners considerable distress (Haupt & Coetzee 2008). Matters came to a head following the 2012 miners' strike at Marikana on the platinum belt, when police shot and killed thirty-four miners. As I noted when discussing the event, newspaper reports pointed out that the miners, not all at the bottom of the pay scale, had unsustainable levels of debt, the automated repayments of which were being facilitated via EAOs. "Shortly after payday . . . many of them simply had nothing left to live on" (James 2015, 63). This tragic event "placed the spotlight squarely and (seemingly) irrevocably on the abuses of the EAO collection system" (Stephan van der Merwe 2021, 58).

In short, this was a virtually unregulated system. In it, undereducated clerks in the country's lowest-level courts were colluding with large commercial lenders by rubber-stamping their requests for automated deductions. Instead of an expensive process using debt collectors, writing lawyers' letters, or threatening legal action, this was a virtually seamless, almost a machine-like method. Furthermore, it was not simply that workers were having their wages docked to repay lenders: there were also systematic abuses to the system. Lenders were having borrowers sign blank forms, forging debtors' signatures, or leaving signatures off altogether (Haupt & Coetzee 2008).

Clerks of the court were issuing orders, paying no attention (as the Marikana case showed) to the number of *other* such orders issued to the same debtor, or—crucially—whether the debtor would be able to afford to live on what remained of his wage. And—in what seemed if not blatantly fraudulent at least extremely cynical—these orders were being requested, and issued, in parts of the country where clerks were known to be most likely to collude, far distant from where the debtor was residing, thus making any appeal expensive or nearly impossible. (This practice was dubbed "forum shopping" during the court case.) Eclipsing all these borderline-illegal procedures, however, was a single, central problem: wage earners or debtors were being overcharged, their debts were being inflated through the addition of debt-collection fees, and deductions directly from debtors' wages through EAOs were enforced despite their having, in many cases, "already paid in excess of what should have been legally due" (Stephan van der Merwe 2021, 67).

These developments, and the observation by Stellenbosch University Law Clinic (SULC) officers that attempting to counter such abuses at the level of individual cases would not deliver the fundamental reform that was needed, set the scene for the courtroom battle. With some support from a wealthy farm owner, Wendy Appelbaum, who had noted with dismay how her own workers' wages were being substantially reduced, a case was brought before the Western Cape High Court. The granting of such orders was extraordinarily widespread and ubiquitous—in the case of one of the applicants in the case, the clerk of the court had "issued three EAOs on the same day attaching almost her entire salary." Those listed as respondents in the case were not only the thirteen lending companies, but also a firm of attorneys that specialized in debt collection on their behalf. This firm had on its books debt to the "total value . . . of R1,597,585,832.00 (that is, over one and a half billion rands)."[3]

Let us skip forward, briefly, to the outcome of the case in that court. The judge condemned, in particular, the systematic abuse of the system. Finding that this had effectively denied the respondents' access to justice, he ruled that the garnishee orders issued against them were "unlawful, invalid and of no force and effect," and declared the relevant section of the Magistrates' Court Act, under which such orders were being issued, to be unconstitutional. His ruling was widely lauded as a milestone in debtor protection by "affording judicial recognition to the rampant abuses associated with the EAO mechanism" and by suggesting "judicially enforceable corrective measures" to prevent such abuses in future (Stephan van der Merwe 2021, 84).

The judge noted a clash between procedures in these low-level regional courts, using the Magistrates' Courts Act in force since 1944,[4] and the rights enforced by the highest forum of justice in the land, the Constitutional Court, born of the country's post-democracy legal order in 1994. For the judgment to carry any force, this court would be required to endorse it. In 2016,[5] the Constitutional Court duly ruled that no such order may be issued without authorization by the court "after satisfying itself that it is just and equitable and that the amount is appropriate," and legislation was subsequently passed—the Courts of Law Amendment Bill (CLA)[6]—to alter the Magistrates Courts Act accordingly.

What Are Wages For?

This, in sparse outline, is a summary of the formal legal procedure on which my story hangs. Behind this much-lauded victory, and underlying the sometimes-unintelligible statements and rulings involved, lies a complex tangle of claims and counter-claims; a struggle between those creditors and lawyers intent on being repaid by using "deductions" and those activists and lawyers intent on curbing such intentions through "counter-deductions." As the arms race played itself out, those fearing that their ready access to repayment would be threatened then hit back by engaging in "counter-counter-deductions." The nub of this contestation concerned a set of machine-like financial arrangements, through which employees' earnings were being diminished in a manner that was beyond their control. And it concerned the way those wages were evaluated or estimated. It also concerned what rights diverse parties enjoyed to access, defend, or plunder those wages.

The circumstances and wages of the fifteen applicants in the case are summarized in Table 3.1. SULC, as the representative of all these individuals, was named as first applicant.[7] It shows that all were in low-paid and/or precarious jobs, indicates the monthly amounts that were being deducted through EAOs, and demonstrates the high amounts required to be repaid compared to the level of income. The list of lenders in the right-hand column shows just how many loans—and lenders—were involved.

Let us look at one of the affidavits in detail in order to understand the convoluted peculiarities of the repayment system. VX, a general worker, states that he is the sole breadwinner, supporting his wife and several children. Wishing to help an elderly relative rebuild her house, he applied to borrow

TABLE 3.1: Applicants in the EAO case

Applicant	Occupation	Wage	EAO Amount	Borrowed	Owes	Lenders
USLAC (now SULC)						
VX	General worker	R2,400.00	R1,519.00		R4,623.56	SA Multiloan/Mavava Trading 279/Cannistraro Investments 275/Onecor/Dotmobile/Flemix/River Bush Property Trust
MA	Lay counselor	R5,000.00	R1,015.17			
AA	Food services assistant		R2,955.96	R7,982.00	R9,035.56	SA Multiloan/Bridge Corporate
LDB	Cleaning assistant					
FB	Cleaning assistant	R7,000.00	R2,200.00	R4,333.17		Utafutaji Trading 83/Aeferno Investments 269/Experato
MB	Cleaning assistant	R2,600.00	R1,395.89			Los Manos/Onecor/Coombe
JK	General worker	R2,300.00	R862.50	R5,200.00		SA Multiloan/Polkadot/Coombe/Experato
SF	Cleaning assistant	R8,000.00	R850.00			SA Multiloan/Moneybox Investments/ Maravedi Credit Solutions/Coombe
JHa	Security guard	R5,000.00	R648.96		R14,215.00	Maravedi/Flemix
JHe	Seasonal worker	R1,200.00	R1,100.00	R4,900.00	R28,903.48	WP Loans/Icom/Coombe/Flemix/Amplisol/Maravedi
DJ	General worker	R2,500.00	R1,200.00	R6,931.00	R11,039.00	SA Multiloans/Villades Roses/Flemix/Bridge Corporate
BM	Maintenance worker	R3,600.00	R670.00			JD/Maravedi
SS	Baker	R2,750.00	R700.00	R1,500.00		SA Multiloans/Moneybox Investments
NT	Unemployed	Nil	R736.71			
DW	Farm worker	R2,600.00	R648.06			River Bush Property Trust

money from a microlender called SA Multiloan, whose agent asked him for a pay slip and three months' bank statements. He later discovered that the loan officer filling in the "affordability assessment" had estimated the family's food bills (in a sleight-of-hand avoiding the legal obligation not to lend an unrepayable amount) at an absurdly low R50 monthly. The loan was paid into his account. Upon defaulting on a second loan from the same company, he learned that a different company, Mavava Trading 279, unknown to him, had obtained an EAO against his salary in a remote magistrate's court. The order was served on his employer, who was ordered to deduct R807 monthly; later a second order was served, similarly instructing a deduction of R722 monthly—both in payment of the amounts owing. In this second case, a variety of intermediary companies was involved, ranging from Cannistraro Investments 275, through Onecor and Dotmobile, to Flemix and River Bush Property Trust. The same magistrates' court had been used, by all of them, to issue the orders.

What is evident is the cascading effect through which the company originally giving the loan was, shortly thereafter, supplanted by a second, third, and even fourth company. This happened either because the loan book was being sold or (as was common in this case) because one company had merged with, turned into, or was even masquerading as another. In other cases, Bridge Corporate or Bridge Group appears to be identical to, and uses the same letterhead and address, as Flemix.[8] Later in the papers, it becomes evident that the debts were, even further down the line, sold on to individual debt collectors.

VX states in his affidavit that, "because of the attachment of almost half" his wages, he was "at that stage literally struggling to put food on the table."[9] The legal battle was, in part, being fought over what wages represent, what they are actually *for*. Summing up later, Judge Desai in his initial judgment in the Western Cape High Court pointed especially to the impact of EAOs on several "constitutionally enshrined human rights" of the debtor and their family: rights to "access to healthcare, food, education, housing, shelter, family life and human dignity." The implication was that by drastically (and mostly with borderline legality) reducing the portion of workers' wages that are necessary to *exercise* those rights, this system of deductions threatened not only those workers' livelihoods but other aspects of their well-being. Any "court order or legislation which deprives a person of their means of support or impairs the ability" to "earn an income and support themselves and their families," said the judge, would limit their "right to dignity" (Stephan van der Merwe 2021, 83).

This judge's statement echoes and summarizes several of those made in the documents and affidavits submitted to the court. Kruger van der Walt, an attorney from SULC, queried

> whether it is constitutionally permissible for a person's wage to be attached without any form of judicial oversight in order to satisfy a judgement debt. This issue has implications and prospective effect for the public in general and in particular the livelihoods and very survival of vulnerable low-income debtors whose wages or salaries are subject to an EAO.

He also stressed how "the basic socio-economic rights required for a human to survive: shelter, electricity, sufficient food, healthcare as well as other rights such as access to education for children are all threatened when a debtor cannot afford" these, because of "the deductions taken from her salary" and when she "lacks the means to challenge the order in the court which issued it." Further on in the documentation, he noted that many of the applicants had EAOs issued against them for amounts of a third to half of their salaries, and pointed out that "money that would otherwise have been spent on food, shelter, medicine, clothing, school fees and other necessities . . . was effectively seized from their salaries without any semblance of a hearing before an independent judicial officer."[10]

In short, it was being argued that debtors ought never to have so much of their wages taken away that they and their families are not left with enough to live on. But the very question of what "enough" actually equated to was itself a matter for assertion, dispute, and speculation. The matter was eventually settled through a reliance on the fixed quality of numbers and of specified percentages. In his retrospective reflections on the case, SULC's Stephan van der Merwe discusses the importance of "proportionality": a legal principle that requires the balancing of conflicting interests (Stephan van der Merwe 2021, 219–227). He argues that South Africa's mixed bag of law, with new systems superimposed on old ones, has resulted in a fundamental vagueness (2021, 27–41). Initially the ruling by Judge Desai left the question of "how much is enough" to "judicial oversight" but later, when the Magistrates' Courts Act was amended, the amount was specified as an exact proportion. Taking into account all possible deductions, no more than a total of 25 percent of a worker's wage ought to be docked in this way.

However, while the court case was in motion and the matter still under discussion, there were disputes over what a wage is for, who has the right to it, and how much of it "is enough." Van der Walt, the SULC attorney, was speaking emotively of all the things a debtor ought to, or might have been, able to buy with her wage, had it not been summarily reduced. Desai's eventual judgment echoed this, ruling that a definite quantity (or proportion) of that wage was essential to its earner, since it represented material needs for food and shelter. Matters were construed very differently in the testimony by Flemix & Associates, the firm of attorneys that—under a variety of guises—had been collecting debts on behalf of the thirteen "credit provider" respondents in the case. Here, debtors' wages—and the accounts into which they were regularly paid—were instead configured as a terrain to which *they,* as creditors, had preferential rights, in order to keep the system going. Not to permit EAOs on debtors' wages, claimed Aletta Flemix, was to deny *creditors'* access to the courts: a deprivation that outweighed that experienced by any debtor. The rationale spelled out in her lengthy affidavit concerned the effects of such a denial on "the entire credit/unsecured lending as well as debt collection industry."[11] There was also the well-worn claim that, by defending that industry, she was ultimately upholding the interests of borrowers (Daniels 2004, 846–847; James 2015, 65). Disallowing these automated deductions, Flemix claimed, would mean "credit would cost much more" and that alternative, "unlawful" methods would be turned to by those unable to meet such costs.

Making a similar claim about the right to deduct—and denying that Flemix and the various intermediaries in the repayment chain were engaged in "forum shopping" when they sought out remote magistrates' courts distant from debtors' domiciles to issue the EAOs—was the plaintive cry by Marius Jonkers, CEO of the Association of Debt Recovery Agents. He pointed out "that the Magistrates' Court, which had jurisdiction" in respect of certain debtors,

> flatly refused to issue judgements . . . while others, due to problems of capacity and a shortage of manpower, were unable to deal, or expeditiously deal, with applications for judgement. . . . As a result it was . . . impossible for credit providers to obtain judgement . . . against the defaulting debtors in such courts, which obviously infringed upon the credit provider's fundamental right of access to court.[12]

Overall, the argument being made by these creditor/respondents was that the ready access they had enjoyed to borrowers' wages and accounts (in part facilitated by their use of uneducated clerks and faraway magistrates' courts) was what had enabled them to keep the cost of credit as low as it was, and that this low rate was, in the end, to the benefit of those borrowers. They did not explicitly address why they had routinely failed to establish how much of these borrowers' wages were required to put food on the table, but the example of VX suggests that some of their loan officers—the foot soldiers of the system— had estimated this, cynically, at unrealistically low amounts.

Visible and Invisible Agents

The affidavits submitted by the various applicants in the SULC case repeatedly make the point that they are mystified about *who* had lent them money and *to whom* it was owed. Some of this was because of the selling of debt and/or the reliance on debt collectors with no apparent connection to the company that originated the loan—both widespread practices in the US, the UK, and beyond (Carruthers 2022).[13] And some of it was the result of a system of internal subdivision that involved the naming and deceptive renaming of companies and/or the parceling off or creation of subsidiary sub-companies with unrelated designations and titles/logos, but otherwise identical paperwork, to the original one.

The selling of debt, in this case, has the effect of concealing the identity of the lender and thus confusing the borrower. Odette Geldenhuys, the instructing attorney on the SULC case, commented on the impersonal character of a system in which a debt is packaged and transferred: "it loses its connection to a real human. It becomes a commodity, it has no relationship to the person who six years ago borrowed the money."[14] A similar argument was evident in the affidavits by debtor/applicants in the case. VX's affidavit states that

> 17. During late 2012, a man whom I do not know came to my work and demanded that I sign some documents; and when I refused to do so he became angry and left. This man was by himself [i.e. alone]. . . . . From these documents I learned that Mavava Trading 279, an entity unknown to me, and from which I have never taken a loan, had obtained an emoluments attachment order against me in the Beaufort West Magistrates' Court during 2012.

> 21. . . . . This form was allegedly signed by Josef Naude . . . . and JC Eksteen. I have never met these people and do not know who they are. If it is alleged that they accompanied the stranger referred to in paragraph 17 above, I deny that.

As this indicates, a bewildering string of companies and sub-companies stood as intermediaries between VX and the originators of the two loans he took out—from SA Multiloan and Dotmobile, respectively. The entity that applied for the EAO following the default on the original loans, here as with the other applicants, was not the one that had lent the money in the first place. Despite being at arms' length, however, these entities were closely connected. Again, the precise character of their relationship was not clear, but it was something that troubled and exercised some of those involved in the case, who even suggested that these links suggested corruption. Bridge Loans (including and/or referred to elsewhere as Bridge Group and Bridge Corporate) was an overarching entity that subsumed several others. Flemix & Associates, directed by Alanza Flemix-Jordaan (referred to elsewhere in the documentation as "Aletta"), was securing EAOs for Onelaw—a company established to trace defaulters on loans.[15] Bridge Loans, I heard from the attorney on the case, had been offering various lenders an investment vehicle whose high returns were guaranteed by the seamless mechanism of debt collection afforded by EAOs. In several of these companies (which seemed to have relatives or close friends as directors), the same finance department and debt-recovery mechanisms were used. The director in all three cases is listed as "Alanza Flemix-Jordaan (LLB)." One affidavit specifies the chain of companies to which debts were being outsourced:

> In terms of a cession agreement concluded between the 14th respondent and Bridge Corporate, . . . the 14th respondent on 13 February 2013 ceded its claim against the 12th applicant to Bridge Corporate. This explains why the name of Bridge Corporate appears as the creditor on the statement relating to the outstanding debt of the 12th applicant. . . . [That claim] has subsequently been ceded by Bridge Corporate to Levina Jacoba Landman.

Other affidavits give similar accounts of an applicant's being accosted, and threatened, by unknown strangers, often acting alone. "A man approached me and threatened me with imprisonment and the loss of my job"; "I was approached at work by a man who forced me to sign some documents"; "A man came to my work in 2012, he tried to get me to agree on a deduction from my debit card but I did not agree on the amount and he left."[16] The fact that the "men" who approached each of the applicants in this case were unknown to them points to an essential aspect of the business model in which debts are sold and thereafter collected by EAOs.

The transfer of debts, like a game of "hot potato," seems to have been seen, overall, as enabling creditors to deny responsibility for reckless lending. Not only were loans sold, but there were also cases in which subsidiaries did the collection; in others the loans were passed down the line to individual debt collectors. The "originator" of a loan, in such cases, sold it on to a second party, which then sold it again to a third one. The third party then hired a collector or resold the debt to him. Then "they say that they're not the judgment creditor. They sold it. So they don't know how their name is here," as I was told by Sune van der Merwe, an employee of Summit Financial Partners, a company that was investigating practices in similar cases of borderline legality. However, she said, having one's name as creditor on an EAO means "you can't really pass the buck. That's legal and that's binding."[17] This process was made more confusing still by the fact that certain debt collectors were no longer working for the firms that once employed them. For example, one collector of debt repayments from four of the applicants, had "subsequently terminated his employment with G Wilson Tracing."[18] Overall, passing debts on enabled a company seeking legitimacy to deny responsibility for behavior that might be considered borderline illegal.

This system of debt selling explains why, when the attorneys were preparing the materials for the case, they were unable to procure original statements of account and similar documents from the original lenders, as several affidavits attest. The loans had been sold. In one case, an affidavit from the administrative team leader at Maravedi Credit Solutions, one of the entities that had bought debts for recovery, states that "attempts to obtain the original documentation from JDG Trading Limited have been unsuccessful. It is not known what happened to the original documentation and after a thorough and diligent search therefor, same appears to be lost, misplaced or destroyed." Clarifying to whom the debt now "belonged," she said "the defendant is therefore indebted to Maravedi Credit Solutions, successor in title to the debt from JDG Trading (Pty) Ltd." and (naming a string of furniture and appliance stores somewhat notorious for selling to low-wage consumers on installment plans and for their relentless collection practices) "as Joshua Doore or Russells or Electric Express or Morkels or Bradlows or Price 'n Pride or Barnetts . . ."[19] Given that the original documentation proved impossible to find, the attorney told me, those preparing the case ended up using "bits of paper, final demands, etc." provided by the applicants. This had knock-on effects on the planning for the trial and its effects: "They began to realize they wouldn't be able to address

the issues of 'reckless lending,' given the lack of paper evidence."[20] It was partly
for this reason that the eventual judgment centered, relatively narrowly, on
two specific abuses of the EAO system: the use of local rather than remote
courts and the importance of proper judicial oversight by a magistrate.

With this, as with other aspects of the EAO system, the familiar refrain was
that of justifying the existing arrangements, since anything involving more
effort would make it necessary to use alternative (more costly or less legal)
methods if this convenient business model were challenged: "Creditors might
resort to extrajudicial processes to collect debts, including unlawful methods." The spokesman for the Association of Debt Recovery Agents (ADRA),
for his part, insisted that they always follow the "code of conduct" and the
rules laid out in the handbook. Flemix, in her affidavit, was maintaining that
her company was such a well-oiled machine that, if anything went wrong, this
could only be at the level of such debt collectors—and that this was "not under
our control." This amounted to an assertion that, "if individuals don't follow
the rules, this is down to them rather than down to us."

Attaching Property, Bodies, or Wages?

Reading these affidavits and interviewing protagonists after the conclusion of
the case, it became clearer why protection of debtors' wages and accounts, on
the one hand, and direct and easy access to them, on the other, had been so crucial. But it is important to acknowledge that this direct and easy access—and
an automated system of docking wages—can be seen, from the wage earner's
perspective, as advantageous in certain circumstances. As economist Jimmy
Roth illustrated, in a study of financial services in an African township, wages
paid directly into employees' bank accounts enable wage earners to "borrow
without collateral" or "use their expected wages as a collateral substitute"
(Roth 2004, 78). In similar vein, automated deductions, if properly regulated,
can be a convenient way to pay a bill: much like a direct debit (Stephan van der
Merwe 2021, 268), it can reduce the need to arrange payments through other,
more convoluted and time-consuming means.

It was, then, the cynically abusive aspects of such deductions, rather than
the system in and of itself, that had been found to be beyond the pale. The
findings of the Constitutional Court, and their later translation into law with
the Courts of Law Amendment Bill (CLA), had an effect that may not have
been immediate but that was marked. Over time, noted various interlocutors,

the outcome of the case meant that the once-seamless process of debt recovery had become more arduous. In order to understand just how arduous, it is instructive to look back at the years before this seamless process had been put in place.

In the two decades before this court case, it had become easy to "attach" wages and then drain them away through the use of EAOs. This process had lessened the need—as was the much earlier practice—to rely on other forms of collateral, notably those of seizing bodies and, later, confiscating property. Reflecting on how this system had evolved, Geoff Budlender, the advocate who had represented SULC in the High Court case, pointed out that getting to the very source of a consumer's ability to purchase the key elements of a livelihood—his wage—was less troublesome to creditors than reclaiming material items later, after the event. The emoluments attachment system was easier to operate than that earlier practice of confiscating assets.

> One is, it's quite expensive. You've got to . . . get a court order, and court process and then get the sheriff. Secondly, it leads to a physical confrontation sometimes, which people don't want to get involved in. Thirdly, what you can get is quite limited: people's furniture. It has a high value to the owners, but it has no value for resale purposes to the creditor. So, I suspect that what you get back is usually peanuts, by the time you've paid the legal fees and the sheriff. . . . then you've got to go and sell the damn stuff at the auctioneer.[21]

By contrast, a wage represents collateral for a "very secure loan, it's the best. Nowhere else can you get it off the top" in the same way, he claimed.

A similar point was made by one Marius Jonker, representing the Association of Debt Recovery Agents (ADRA) in his court affidavit in the SULC case. In defense of the existing EAO procedures, he argued that they

> provide time-saving and cost effective procedures for credit providers to collect debts in an unsecured lending environment. . . . These . . . are also beneficial to debtors for the aforesaid reasons (as the costs involved in these processes are ultimately carried by the debtor) and because it avoids the attachment of the debtor's assets.

Attaching assets, he and others testified, was costly and time-consuming. It entailed a drawn-out procedure that potentially resulted in great inconvenience and loss (to the debtor, he stressed) whose assets are sold in execution. These "do not provide viable alternatives to be used on a large scale."[22]

Behind this most recent development lay over a century of earlier judicial experiments enabled through a kind of palimpsest that involved a set of overlapping legal orders. South Africa's approach to the withholding of wages is the result of a complex combination of some of these.[23] In the early days at the Cape, a Roman Dutch law regime was used. English common law was adopted following the annexation of the Cape and then Natal by the British in the early nineteenth century, and through the establishment, in the early twentieth, of the Union of South Africa as a dominion of the British empire. This uneven combination of judicial systems enabled the gradual replacement of the bodily seizure and imprisonment of debtors by the attachment of their salaries: a way of confiscating property as a substitute for arresting the debtor. Such a system was already widespread in the territory in the early years of the twentieth century (Stephan van der Merwe 2021, 38–39) and was eventually enshrined in the Magistrates' Courts Act of 1944: a piece of legislation modeled on a British precedent. But this attachment of salaries would initially have applied more to white persons of British/European heritage than to the minority of black people who, at that time, aspired to a middle-class lifestyle and/or who owned property. In the case of the latter, who were more-or-less excluded from mainstream legal and financial arrangements, creditors were forced to arrive in person rather than taking repayments from "Native" (that is, black African) debtors' earnings. In the 1930s, social worker Ray Phillips quoted a black pastor, Rev. Henry M. Nawa, who was experiencing difficulty collecting overdue church fees from his congregants:

> When you come to get the fees you find the furniture man who wants to collect and other Native men to whom money is owing and to whom promises have been made. The ones who come first get the money, the rest are put off with various promises until a later time. (1938, 40)

Between that date and the 2000s, when EAOs were affecting many lives and livelihoods, black workers had been brought within the embrace of the garnishee order system, although still excluded from the more beneficial aspects of access to credit and borrowing. That is to say, they were suffering from the punitive dimension of the credit/legal complex while unable to benefit fully from its advantages.

In the 1980s, however, the harsh punishments faced by (especially black) debtors could, in fact, still involve imprisonment, as Geoff Budlender pointed out.

What we were fighting then was not so much emolument attachments as arrests for non-payment of debt. . . . You would get brought before court, under what was then section 65 of the Magistrate's Court Act. You would get ordered by the court to pay in instalments and then, when you didn't pay, you would be arrested, not for not paying the debt but for contempt of court, for not complying with the court order. Because we don't have civil imprisonment for debt. Most countries don't have that any longer. But the theory was, this *wasn't* civil imprisonment for debt.[24]

Such imprisonment, in the 1990s, was found by the court to be inconsistent with the right to personal freedom that was enshrined in the (then draft) constitution.[25] As a result, certain clauses in Section 65 of the Magistrates' Courts Act were found to be invalid. Others, however, were left in place—and continued to underpin the garnishee system up to the time of the SULC Constitutional Court case of 2016. Debtors' bodies were no longer subject to seizure, and their property, as Budlender says, was insufficient to make confiscation worthwhile. But what debtors did have was wages, and it was the race to secure the biggest possible share of these—by creditors, lawyers such as Flemix, and others—whose results the court case had adjudicated.

Following the Victory: The Arms Race Continues

In the aftermath of the Constitutional Court ruling, further steps were needed for that ruling to be put into effect. But its general drift became known within the wider world of debt recovery. Many of my interlocutors indicated that there was soon a marked drop in the issuing of garnishee orders. Those charged with recovering debt, the lawyers representing them, and a range of new actors in the field had to find other ways of recouping unpaid debts: of upping the ante.

As news of the case spread, the EAO ceased to be used as a *modus operandi*. Its shortcomings—including the failure to accurately estimate the appropriate proportion of a borrower's wage that ought to remain and be available to support his livelihood and the indiscriminate use of faraway courts and undereducated and compliant clerks—meant that those making a living from lending and debt collection needed to find new ways to achieve the same ends: to continue making "deductions" from wage earners' bank accounts. In some cases they pursued (and their opponents challenged) this search through the courts. In others, distinctly non-legal and fraudulent means were used to achieve the same ends.

Legal Means

This continued struggle saw the increased involvement of private actors beyond the world of the university law clinics. These included businessmen operating on behalf of large employers. One of them, Clark Gardner, CEO of Summit Financial Partners, made it the task of his firm to create the conditions for a better-regulated form of capitalism. A subsidiary called Q-Link was charged with this task. Taking the form of a kind of corporate social responsibility, Q-Link's efforts were made partly at the behest of, and paid for by, large mining consortia that were running scared in the wake of events like the trade union protest at the Marikana mine, where miners demanding higher pay turned out to have been forfeiting most of their wages to high-interest lenders via automatic deductions. Anglo American, Lonmin, and Amplats, among other companies, wished to secure a more sustainable form of livelihood for their workers, allowing a sufficient proportion of their pay to remain for their own and their families' use. To this end, Q-Link began to undertake "payroll administration."

What Gardner and his officers were combatting, he told me, is an attitude that views workers' wages—or "wallets"—as something to be "taken." To illustrate, he imagined himself as a debt collector:

> if I don't take your wallet, your full wallet, someone else is going to take it. If you can afford R100 a month on debt installments, I want to take that full hundred. Because if I take R80, someone else is going to take the other R20. That is putting my loan at risk. And no one is policing that. So I can do whatever I want. So the lack of enforcement has actually created a reckless lending environment. If you don't play that game you're going to lose. It's like in cycling, if you don't take the drugs that everyone else is taking, you're going to be left behind. In South Africa, the more manipulative and unscrupulous you were the better you did. And people were forced to play that game . . .[26]

A member of his investigative team, Sune van der Merwe, talked me through some of the cases she was looking into as part of an attempt to counter this free-for-all with workers' wages. Confirming that the SULC case had now made it difficult to get a garnishee order, she also acknowledged that the alternative of attaching property was of little use, because "most of these people don't own anything. . . . Debt collectors have thus reverted to 'soft collection' instead—phoning and pestering until they get someone to sign their debit order authorization."

Regrettably, but perhaps predictably, such forms of pestering can assume the form of a promise of a loan as a helpful solution to indebtedness. In one case, there was an online company purporting to be a loan facilitation platform.

> *Sune:.* . . . when you fill in all your details, thinking that you're going to apply for a loan, you've signed up for their service package. Which you are unaware of until you suddenly get a debit order of R450, and then R99 for the rest of the year.
>
> *Deborah:.* What does that service package involve?
>
> *Sune:.* It's apparently legal advice. Which is also something that is shocking. It says that it will give you litigation advice, domestic violence advice. Things that these people obviously don't sign up for. A client came back to us. He figured out he had it, he disputed the debit orders, and now these people are sending him unissued summonses, saying that, "We're going to . . . blacklist you. You're going to have a judgment against your name." Forcing the person to pay the full amount for the service package that he never even knew that he was taking out. It's unbelievable.[27]

One of the things that came to light in the course of the "payroll administration" undertaken by Q-Link was an ambiguity in what was permissible as "collection costs." This ambiguity had been exploited by a firm of attorneys based near the site of South Africa's platinum belt, where Lonmin and Amplats operate their mines and where Marikana is situated. "The way the payments work," Sune told me, is "you first pay your collection costs, then you pay your legal fees, then you pay interest. Then, only, you pay capital," Many workers end up never paying off the original loan—"you're going to have this unending amount of . . . collection fee, that people are going to end up paying back forever." Although the court case had newly established a regulatory framework as noted above, fees charged by lawyers through the EAO mechanism had been excluded from this. In one case involving said attorney, shows lawyer Stephan van der Merwe in his account of the matter,

> even though interest was capped at an amount equal to the original debt of R1,900, the collection of the debt had attracted legal fees, expenses and VAT in excess of R7,300. After already collecting R8,800 through an EAO, the creditor alleged that the debtor still owed R2,365, which was more than the initial loan amount. (Stephan van der Merwe 2021, 111)

The reason why this particular attorney's office was "opposing the matter," explained Sune, was not that they objected to changing the law *in the future* to include legal fees in the total amount allowed for collection via the EAO mechanism. Rather, it was their fears about having to *pay back* all the money they had *already* amassed through debt collection in the past.

When this case came to court, a year after my conversation with Sune, the seemingly unregulated addition of lawyers' fees to "collection costs" (i.e., costs of pursuing the collection of debts) was challenged.[28] The applicants, including mining giant Lonmin on behalf of its employees, maintained that legal fees should form part of the definition of collection fees and be regulated in the same way. The applicants submitted that "vulgar and immoral" addition of legal costs to cover debt collection (but in fact vastly exceeding those required for such a purpose) were the rule rather than the exception. As it turned out, the applicants' case was dismissed with costs, but on technical grounds, a decision that Stephan van der Merwe saw as "regrettable" since the court "failed to apply itself to the merits of the applicants' arguments" (2021, 117).[29] A passionate defender of the rights of low-wage debtors, van der Merwe argued that "some of these EAOs may arguably have been granted lawfully but were now being abused as vehicles of unlawful collections" (Stephan van der Merwe 2021, 118). Being permitted indiscriminately to add lawyers' fees, he showed, meant that lenders would never be held to account for failing to assess borrowers' ability to repay before lending them money in the first place. (The affordability test would be calculated only on the loan itself, not taking these extra fees into account.) The ruling allowing "no more than 25 percent" of a wage to be withheld from its earner via an EAO would thus become risible and of no effect.

This and similar questions continued to be pursued through the courts. A subsequent case procured a judgment that favored distressed and low-wage debtors and ruled against creditors that continued irresponsibly to "run up legal costs with no regard for consumers."[30] The case, again involving SULC, seemed to turn the tables on the creditors. The judge stated that

> If equality requires all persons an equal right to access to credit but con-
> sumers are not equal in their ability to pay then it must equally mean that
> the cost of credit must be adapted accordingly. In reality the converse has
> happened and the cost of credit for small loans is disproportionately higher
> than for large loans. (cited in Stephan van der Merwe 2021, 131)

No sooner had the judge ruled in favor of the low-paid applicants in this case, however, than leave to appeal was sought.[31] The arms race over access to workers' wages continued.

Public Service Employees: Illegal Means

Following the SULC judgment of 2017 that made "lawful" EAOs more diffi-cult to procure, Clark Gardner's Summit Financial and Q-Link noticed some much less formal—and frankly fraudulent—ways in which workers' wages were being pilfered. In the course of their work on payroll administration on PERSAL (Personnel and Salary System), through which the payment of public service employees is centrally administered, they discovered three companies—Self-Discovery, Creative Upliftment, and Self Reliance—that had authorized a suspicious number of EAO deductions coming off the pay slip of specific employees. Upon investigation, they discovered that these, along with sixteen others, all had their headquarters in the same building and that "a lot of the founding directors of the companies, or their . . . members, were past or current employees of government."[32] Summit unveiled that these companies had fraudulently issued EAOs using case numbers that had been allocated to completely different public service employees: "they are committing fraud . . . until they can prove otherwise, by falsifying case numbers." They had possibly stolen an official court stamp or forged one, making it look as though these orders had been approved by the clerk of the court, had served these papers on the employer (in this case the government), and were deducting amounts of money from the salaries of the employees in question. For one such company, Sune reported that they investigated nineteen EAOs, all of which were found to be fraudulent. These "companies" were not able to prove that the orders were valid, or that they had indeed been processed through a magistrates' court. The companies had tried to fight Q-Link on legal points alone, trying to blame the error on the clerk of the court. Q-Link's response, putting them out on a limb in terms of strict legal procedure, had been to go to the court and request a suspension of all these EAOs. The court had agreed—pending further investigation—to do so, "because it potentially affects a large population of government employees, and it is potentially fraud."

What these stories reveal—whether they concern legal and court-related systems or illegal ones that mimic or mirror court-based ones—is the impor-tance of retaining the facility of access to employees' wages. To do so is to be able to tap into a rich seam of resources (if possible, even what Gardner called a "full wallet," leaving none for other looters), something that will not be given up without a struggle. The closing-off of the route through which this was earlier accomplished, itself a borderline-illegal one, has had the effect of pushing agents towards equally suspect alternatives.

The net result for employees, whether they work for big mining companies or in the public service, has been to diminish the proportion of the remuneration they earn that is available to "put food on the table," in the words of VX in the SULC case, or to access "healthcare, . . . education, housing, shelter, family life and human dignity," in the words of the judge who presided over that case. We should bear in mind Stephan van der Merwe's highlighting of "proportionality"—a legal principle that requires the balancing of conflicting interests. It seems here that such a balance—answering the question "how much is enough" to purchase food, access healthcare, or safeguard the other rights enumerated by the judge—must be ensured through pitched battles between those aiming to make a higher such proportion available to wage earners themselves and those seeking to lessen that proportion by making it fair game for deductions. In sum, in answer to the question "What are wages for?" the answer is being endlessly contested.

Workers' Wages: Autonomy or Protection?

I noted earlier how unsecured loans proliferated in post-democracy South Africa. They were "unsecured" because in most cases the borrowers had little in the way of fixed property. According to Clark Gardner, with his claim to be pursuing a fairer, more equitable capitalism, some of the problem lay in a historical anomaly that had denied most black people, during apartheid, the right to own real estate. Some of these loans were accruing interest

> at 100% pa. If they could use the equity in their title deeds they would learn to use it responsibly—and borrow at 13%. You would have a few burnt out, but at least there would be some sort of security.[33]

Owning property, however precariously, is seen here as enabling fairer interest rates. Such ownership has also been viewed in the literature as potentially providing some basis for political action to counter the powers of the credit industry. In a 1970s social movement in the United States, neighborhood residents reimagined the deposits they had made into banks and lending institutions as "owned" by them—thus challenging the power of those lenders to control the situation (Krippner 2017, 11–13). In the present case, what was owned was—or should have been—the wages earned. These served as a "collateral substitute" (Roth 2004, 78),[34] which ought, by rights, to have made for more affordable rates of interest. The battle was one between those defending earners' ownership of, and right to control, the fruits of their labor, and those seeking—and convinced that it was their right to have ready access to—the earnings of others in order to conduct their business and to enhance their bottom line.

Perhaps a glaringly obvious point concerns the responsibility of the borrower/wage earner herself. In the story told here, the disputants on both sides of the fray appear to be acting *on behalf* of that earner; there is little discussion of the worker's part in defending her wages unaided. The need to educate potential debtors about the dangers of borrowing too much, and the importance of "financial literacy" and/or frugality have been much discussed (James et al. 2020; Lazarus 2020; Ndumo 2011). These discussions have their place, but it is important to realize that the factors that have combined to produce South Africa's debt epidemic are largely structural and that the actions of any particular wage earner or debtor are able to have only a limited effect. It is also important to note that, within an overarching framework that has almost overdetermined the high amount of unsecured lending, many people want to continue borrowing regardless of the results: "People are pressurized by competition in the township[;] if someone has something, someone else will want to have [it], without considering the cost," one interlocutor told me (James 2015, 45). On occasion, attempts to intervene on wage earners' behalf, by restricting what can be done to their wages, encounter resistance, not only from seemingly rapacious creditors but from those earners themselves. In some of the cases taken on by Summit and Q-Link, they have attempted to pursue the interests of the debtor, approaching the courts in order to challenge the creditor's practices. What stands in the way is that borrowers who find themselves "stuck at the end of the month" might want to borrow once again, as Gardner told me. Approaching the same lender again, such borrowers will find that lender trying to dissuade them from taking the case further with Summit: "if you go back and cancel [your case] with Summit, and sign here, I'll give you your R2,000. And I won't even charge you interest this month."

If this is the case, it is worth considering the question that I put to Clark Gardner: "Are there any good guys out there doing responsible lending as they should? Or is this simply no space for a moral type of lender?" His answer was instructive:

> Imagine that's your job—the more harm you do, the more readily you are going to get your money. Because if I have a portfolio of ten credit providers, and the consumer can afford to pay six, how do I get myself up the priority chain? I have got to somehow get a preferred debit order, I have got to see and track your bank deposits, and steal my bit first, . . . I have got to phone you on Saturday mornings. The more ruthless I am, the better I am going to be a lender. So it is like asking me, do you know a drug dealer that does a good job? And one can actually see unsecured credit as addictive. . . . We can't change the behavior of the consumer, we can only change the behavior of the service provider. . . . So, the first question is, is unsecured credit at all healthy for society? I would say, I think it does a lot more harm than good. Which is why I am fighting the World Bank and IMF, in saying that financial inclusion is great for a country. It is great for a country, it is great for corporate SA. Very harmful, though, for consumers.[35]

There are echoes here of his statement, quoted earlier: "if I don't take your wallet, your full wallet, someone else is going to take it." This suggests a particular cast of mind, not only in answer to the question "what are wages for?" but also "to whom do they rightfully belong?" And it raises questions counterposing individual autonomy, on the one hand, with paternalistic protection, on the other, as noted in the introduction to this chapter.

The counterposing of the two as almost irreconcilable opposites is a key theme running through the story told here. It is reminiscent of what was discussed in Chapter 2. On the one hand, any citizen is deemed to have the right to take control of and "own" her own finances. Preventing her from using these finances as she pleases—including alienating them by agreeing to repurpose them as collateral for loans—would be seen as exercising undue paternalism and denying the "right to property" that had been newly affirmed in the constitution during the democratic transition. On the other, failing to specify the percentage of that worker's income that ought *not* to be used in this way can be seen as amounting to neglect. Whether the individual worker/debtor ought to be left to her own devices, in the interests of freedom and autonomy, or whether the wider system—either the law courts or the employer—ought to protect her and be held accountable for such protection, is a question that lies at the heart of this chapter and this book.

Conclusion

The chief relevance of this story for the book concerns the debate over workers' wages, how they relate to debt, what they are for (especially in a setting where permanent or "proper jobs" are increasingly scarce and where wage work is not only low paid but may be of short duration), and to whom they belong. A 2024 newspaper report titled "Past Sins Come Back to Haunt Microlenders" and using evocative terms like "fair settlement" and "restitution," shows that the case, and these questions, have continuing relevance a decade later. Given the somewhat restricted remit of the Constitutional Court case and its failure to restore lost earnings to debtors in individual cases, a small commercial firm has recently been helping challenge specific EOAs in the court. The firm instructs attorneys to take on EOA cases brought by debtors, risking incurring legal fees in the expectation of a cost order from the court. If successful (as they have been in several cases), the firm

> subtracts expenses and the remainder is split 50/50, making it possible for debtors to win back some of what they paid via unlawfully obtained garnishee orders. These are meaningful sums for low-wage debtors who paid lenders significant portions of their earnings for years.[36]

Such challenges to the power of unruly lenders exemplify an important theme in the book. The possibility of clawing back money unfairly repaid embodies some form of recompense for losses suffered as a result of earlier wrongs: some form of redistribution.

How much, then, is enough? When, following the SULC case, the Magistrates' Court Act was amended to specify the maximum proportion—25 percent—of a worker's earnings that may be attached through an EAO, this amounted to an assumption about disposable income. It specified what might be left to that worker, after repaying debts, in order to buy all the bare essentials of life. But if, as in the cases outlined here, low-paid workers need *borrowed* money to procure these, it would seem that the wage, by definition, is too low. (The process of setting out a minimum wage in 2015 was fiercely debated, with some arguing that setting it too high would necessarily be accompanied by "job destruction." The stark choice seemed to be between fewer jobs at higher wages and more jobs at lower ones (Nattrass & Seekings 2014).)

If numerical calculations about monies earned can have such weighty implications, what might it mean to explore the percentage specified by the rewritten Magistrates' Courts Act and assess its implications for one of the applicants? Let us try to calculate the sums (see Table 3.1) for applicant FB, a cleaning assistant. She earns a salary of R7,000. To that, one would need to add the R4,333.17 that she borrowed from various lenders (assuming these were the only loans she took out). Repayments for these, given that this was before the ruling, would likely far exceed the 25 percent that would be permissible to attach through the EAO to enable debt repayments. Doing this kind of calculus could, in the end, lead one into an infinite regress of numbers, percentages, and repayments. Using a social calculus instead, one should perhaps consider what percentage of the wage is necessary for dignity. Is "dignity" an umbrella term under which more easily measured items nestle, or is it something tacked on after all these have been added up? Is it something vague and contextually defined, with any attempt to pin down its exact numerical meaning likely to invite counterclaims (see Marks forthcoming), as was effectively occurring in the courtroom wrangle outlined here? Or does dignity reside, instead, in the ability to decide for oneself what to do with one's wage, rather than having protective arrangements foisted onto one?

Here we might reconsider the topic of financialization and recollect its link to the theme of this book: redistribution. The garnishee order court case features, as respondents, a string of lending companies with oddball names, alongside the firm of attorneys ensuring the collection of their debts. But this should not obscure from view the identity of those large companies glossed in the affidavit as "Joshua Doore or Russells or Electric Express or Morkels or Bradlows or Price 'n Pride or Barnetts." These had earlier been notorious for selling furniture and appliances to low-wage consumers on installment and for their relentless collection practices. Many of them, intensifying their decades-old system of extractive lending facilitated by semi-automated techniques of deduction, have now diversified or switched tack to become financial lenders, finding ever-easier ways of tapping into borrowers' wages to exact repayments while outsourcing debt collection to subsidiaries or independents. The activities of such companies have long been dependent on, and inextricably entangled with, the wages earned, consumption undertaken, and debts paid (and unpaid) by householders.

But to typecast this as yet another case of financialized capitalism, with the state enabling profiteering by big business, would be to simplify the situation. We also need to recognize historical precedents, such that those intent on countering automated forms of extraction echo the earlier paternalism of the colonial authorities that clamped down on nineteenth-century traders' "advances." And we need to understand how, faced with such systematic abuses, people seeking some protection have relied on the human rights legal fraternity and the constitution which that fraternity helped to create. The actions of that fraternity were facilitated by the redistributive tendencies of a newly installed democratic dispensation, such that—at least in the early days of that transition—elite profits and state resources have been channeled and found their way into the pockets of the rank and file.

This chapter has emphasized the formalities and evidentiary systems of the law and of constitutional arrangements, rather than the localized activities of brokers or advisers. It is to the latter topics that I turn in Chapter 4, focusing on the UK.

FOUR

Funding Advice
Patchworks and Boundaries

IN EUROPEAN SETTINGS, recent shifts towards austerity, fiscal citizenship, and financialization have reconfigured the relation among state, market, and charity (Narotzky 2020), changing the nature of wage employment, the character of the welfare state, and the extent to which borrowing money has become imperative (Koch & James 2022). In such settings, advice given by intermediaries is of increased importance to people who must cobble together a living from multiple sources. But those intermediaries do not simply promote strategies for household survival. They, and especially the broader institutions in which their work is done, must secure funds to enable that work to continue. They do so through a process that I and my co-author Caitlin Zaloom have elsewhere called "patchworking." Advisers—with differing status and diverse levels of expertise—act to "identify what resources are available and how they might be accessed, arranged, accounted for, and weighed" (Zaloom & James 2023).

This chapter, then, analyzes the importance of patchwork funding and the advice that it enables. It focuses on the case of the UK. Before doing so, it is important briefly to note, by contrast, how advice is funded and provided in South Africa. In Chapter 3 I noted the role of both the human rights legal fraternity (with its pursuit of constitutional values such as dignity) and of private companies with corporate social responsibility programs (with their interest in establishing a better-regulated form of capitalism). Actors in both sectors stepped up to fill the gap as donations to rights charities by overseas humanitarian and church-based organizations dwindled after the country's transition to democracy. In addition, there are advice services, provided by the Community Advice Office Sector under the rubric of a body called CAOSA, which have national (but geographically uneven) coverage and which rely on piecemeal funding that requires continual reapplication by its recipients. Often in partnership with these offices, Black Sash and similar organizations have been offering guidance and help in many areas, as have trained or trainee lawyers in some university law clinics. But debt advice—the concern of part of this chapter—has been more problematic. "Debt counseling" was construed as an income-generating activity and outsourced to often poorly prepared entrepreneurs (James 2015, 62, 71, 94; Schraten 2014, 11), rather than being furnished centrally, funded by large financial companies, and provided free to debtors, as discussed below for the UK.

Let us turn, then, to the latter: the chief concern of this chapter. Here, a "mixed economy," prevalent for more than a century in the funding and administering of welfare (Cunningham 1998), has become even more dominant in recent times. This mixed economy involves a "pluralist hybrid of market, non-market (e.g. redistribution by the welfare state) and non-monetary (based on reciprocity) forms of economy" (Alexander 2010; see James 2020, 196). Advisers, situated at the interstices of these different sectors, deploy their expertise and mediatory abilities in several important ways, each of which combines nimble flexibility with attentiveness to formal precision. Firstly, they aid their clients in sifting through the complex bureaucracies involved in accessing state welfare funds or in crafting agile responses to demands for often excessive repayments from creditors. By seeking the means "to guide strapped families through financial possibilities, they also *establish distinctions* among the sources they draw together" (my emphasis), thus assisting their clients in "categorizing resources and assigning them as belonging to either households, governments, banks, or others" (Zaloom & James 2023). Secondly, they, and the organizations in which they work, are crucially involved in stitching together the "patches" from novel sources that must be relied on as state backing is increasingly withdrawn. While this involves similar processes of boundary maintenance, since each stream of funding comes with a specific designation and set of conditionalities, it also requires an ability to *combine* these fragments for pragmatic or performative effect.

Analyzing and discussing the funding streams of the advice organizations themselves—how they are viewed, handled, and manipulated—might not normally be thought of as the remit of anthropology, nor yet as an important aspect of redistribution. But, with the flow of state funding reduced to a trickle and with organizations forced to seek alternative sources, the acts of finding, allocating, channeling and diverting funds, and accounting for these, have become a crucial part of what advisers do, and a key consideration for the organizations in which they work. Ingenuity is needed to navigate the restrictions, conditionalities, audits, and red tape, and sometimes it seems that funding strategies loom even larger than the advice itself. Hence the importance of this topic for my book—it is yet another way in which funds need to be clawed back.

The values that motivate and orient advisers are akin to those discussed by Laura Bear and Nayanika Mathur in their account of the "new public good." This is a slippery and often contradictory-sounding phenomenon that combines the unlikely bedfellows of "fiscal discipline, marketization, consensus, transparency and decentralization." Although these are "linked to new technical mechanisms of accountability," the ways they work cannot be captured by "economists' models or the analysis of audit techniques alone" (Bear & Mathur 2015, 20). In a process that might seem counterintuitive, market forces and financialized capitalism, even as some of their logics and agents may appear to be exploiting people or plunging them into debt, also provide funds to ensure that welfare arrangements are maintained and kept in place—as will be demonstrated in the following.

"Problem Clusters"

In the UK, the principal focus of this chapter, the role of advisers has become ever more essential. The need for such advice is, of course, not new. For decades, and especially since the inception of the welfare state, its beneficiaries have needed help to unpack and make sense of the complex elements on which their livelihoods are built. But the need for advice has intensified in the last few decades, owing to welfare reforms that have cut state funding in the name of austerity (see Chapter 1). These have left "everyday life for many ever more precarious" (McDermont 2013), at the same time that the resources to fund advice services are dwindling (Forbess & James 2017).

The entangled constellations of issues with which welfare beneficiaries have been confronted have been described as "problem clusters" by sociolegal scholars (Genn 1999; Moorhead & Robinson 2006; Pleasence et al. 2004). These correspond more or less with the three interconnected sources of livelihood discussed in this book—wages, welfare, and debt. The use of the term "clusters" suggests an embroiled tangle, the solution to which must, of necessity, involve pulling apart the component parts. And, in the process, advisers help clients both demarcate resources as separate from one another and then reunite them. What prompts a person to seek help can appear to consist of just one of these strands. Often it is not the most serious, but it is the one that causes them most fear or anxiety. "People will come in with one issue, but it usually turns out to be several," noted adviser Yusuf.[1] Adviser–advisee encounters involve a thorough sifting through of materials in search of, often, a single all-important document or one crucial detail that, if left undetected, would undermine the fine balance between constantly readjusted sets of income and outgoings. There is a checking of letters, a looking and re-looking through files, and a noting of income, benefits, and budgets. The adviser seeks, then, to compartmentalize problems, but without ignoring the intersections that cause them to "cluster" together. These intersections shape, and are shaped by, the complex interdependencies of householding, but knowing when to pull them (and keep them) apart is key to the boundary work that advisers do. And, in turn, as noted above, advisers also know how and when to recombine these elements, creating a holistic picture of the householders' quandaries and recognizing them as whole people with families.

One key distinction that advisers and advice agencies must make is that which separates welfare issues (here framed as "benefits advice," though these often encompass work-related topics too) from matters relating to indebtedness (framed as "debt advice"). The boundary drawn here operates at multiple levels. In a face-to-face encounter with a client, the benefits adviser lists the client's expenses and establishes what her income is. This includes ascertaining which welfare payments the client is receiving (and at what levels), suggesting others that might supplement that income, and liaising with agencies that may have failed to fulfill their obligations in providing these. If the client turns out to owe money, whether to a commercial creditor or a state agency for "overpaid" benefits (see Chapter 5), she will then be referred to a debt adviser or a specialist debt advice organization. Being transferred across this boundary means the client has the help of an expert who will liaise with the creditor, or lending institution, in order to agree on a schedule of repayments known as a debt management plan. Referral "upwards" or "sideways" is a key element of these arrangements, with advice-giving organizations often required, by their funders, to fulfill specific targets in this respect.

The separation between the two types of advice extends all the way from these local-level encounters upwards to the two distinct sets of funding arrangements that make each of them possible. This neat bifurcation, however, is blurred by the fact that each of these two streams, in turn, is patched together from a complex set of resources. As the next section demonstrates, each—whether "debt" or "benefits" advice—has its own revenue sources, and both have been affected by the cuts in government spending that were heralded by the official adoption of austerity policies in 2010. While attempts to make up the shortfall have, in both cases, continued to involve a "mixed economy" (Cunningham 1998) or "pluralist hybrid" (Alexander 2010), the sources of these mixed and mingled flows of money differ in important respects.

Funding Benefits and Generalist Advice

The introduction of market-oriented policies and regimes has accompanied, and indeed been central to, the cutting of government spending in the UK.[2] These twin processes have amounted to a hollowing out of the welfare state and a further encroachment of mixed or pluralist arrangements as the boundaries between the public and private domains become ever more blurred (Clarke & Newman 1997). The effects of such policies have been decried for several reasons. One is the obvious material effects when these cuts affect welfare benefits. Another is the way the associated audit regimes tie up officers of both public and civil society and charitable organizations in seeking new resources to pay for their work or in justifying their actions through tangled bureaucracy—rather than leaving them free to attend to the more substantive aspects of their jobs. As lifelong advice campaigner Andy Benson summarized it:

> If the state . . . decides it no longer wishes to support professionally based advice work and won't pay for that—what is going to happen? How are people and communities going to gain access to knowledge of their rights and access to redress when things go wrong?[3]

Reform: Audit and Cost Cutting

The "audit culture" (Strathern 2000) that was an intrinsic part of this new funding regime requires some discussion here. Neoliberal discourses have rendered, almost as a kind of common sense, the assumption that welfare reform was required because of the centralized command-and-control approach, and lack of fiscal discipline, of the UK's welfare state.[4] "Reform" was begun by the Thatcher and Major administrations in the 1980s and 90s when they introduced market-based interventions such as New Public Management (NPM), including audits and targets, in an attempt to control local authority financial support for the voluntary sector. Such interventions were aimed at replacing the "presumed inefficiency of hierarchical bureaucracy with the presumed efficiency of markets" (Power 1999, 43).[5] In a parallel move, the voluntary sector faced increased competition from private firms. Council-funded activities like advocacy and counseling are said to have been undermined—as was the independence of the sector as a whole (Gladstone 1999).

This move was further entrenched under New Labour in the 1990s (Patrick 2017). After its election in 1997, the New Labour government added new forms of audit, targets, and more stringent top-down planning while continuing to encourage free-market innovation (Moorhead 2004).[6] An ambitious top-down reform of the system attempted to create economies of scale and a competitive advice market, by bringing local authority-funded advice under central government control, opening legal aid funding to generalist advice agencies, and seeking to integrate specialist and generalist advice into tight-knit partnerships known as CLACs (Community Legal Advice Centres) and CLANs (Community Legal Advice Networks).

It was the second of these reforms that emphasized quality audit. Poor quality advice, it was argued, could do more harm than good. A system was developed whereby

> you had to pass many organization quality assurances to get a franchise and get legal aid.... You had to show you had processes and procedures, an office manual with processes for reviewing and supervising, and show they were being implemented.... But it was very bureaucratic and I don't know if it was always audited intelligently.[7]

These moves sought to bring together two different streams of advice funding: from central government through the legal aid budget, and from the local authority to pay for local civil society organizations offering general advice and information. At the time when a "market-based approach to reform" was proposed (Carter 2006), Matrix Research estimated "the size and nature of the civil and family legal advice sector in England and Wales," revealing that "the advice sector was worth around £5–7 billion, of which nearly two thirds was accounted for by not-for-profit organisations" (Carter 2006, 44). NGO advice work dominated specific areas of the law such as welfare benefits and debt, while solicitors dominated areas like family law. The largest funders of NGO advice were local authorities, but Lord Carter (2006, 45) complained about their disparate aims, saying that they "each have different priorities, funding different types and levels of service, depending on local needs." The most recent reforms, under the Coalition government of 2010 and later the Conservative government of 2015, circumscribed legal aid funds even further and made yet another body—the Legal Aid Agency—responsible for their disbursement.

These new schemas, aimed at the interrelated yet contradictory-seeming goals of free-market-oriented innovation and centrally planned rationality, often generated unforeseen consequences and problems, which in turn required further reform (Power 1999, 27). One of these was to establish, or intensify, the grounds for conflict between local authorities and central government. Indeed, the structural tension between the two has been a key driving force in advice innovation by the former. Charged with the provision of certain key services that are partly funded by local rates and taxes, local authorities have found themselves often paying for or even offering advice as part of that mission, while central government has a history of trying to rationalize advice, make it more efficient and market-driven, and even—under the austerity regime—cut it back altogether. Offering advice in this way enabled local authorities indirectly to claim more resources from central government. They did this by enabling low-wage or unemployed people to glean all the welfare benefits funding to which they were entitled. In this way, they were able to avoid evicting council tenants who fell behind on their rents, collect priority debts they were owed (council tax and rents), and avoid having to provide emergency funding to rescue families from homelessness and destitution (which, as statutory providers, they were obliged by law to do).

Local authorities, themselves squeezed by funding cuts, have thus had to become more proactive in shaping the nature of advice services—partly out of empathy but also as a way of maximizing their own income. By "forcing disparate state agencies to work together" (Forbess & James 2014, 73), multi-focused initiatives undertaken by local authorities have addressed the needs of particularly vulnerable recipients of welfare benefits, while simultaneously ensuring that they are not left out of pocket.

Overall, the net result of the creeping and ever-intensifying emphasis on driving down costs, according to some, has been to put the needs of users ever further from view. Their effect seems to have been to impose on the advice services a culture of entrepreneurialism, with strict rules of financial account-ability and productivity, where these were ill-suited.

From Grants to Commissions and Contracts

Alongside the general reduction in subsidies for advice, a further key devel-opment (and shift from the earlier approach) has been the switch from grants to commissioning. Advice organizations that were once given block grants to fund advice as they saw fit—a model that they preferred since it allowed them to design the services they recognized as necessary—were forced into new con-tract and commissioning arrangements. Under this new public procurement regime, commissioners specify how the service should be run and demand evidence of value for money (Gladstone 1999, 88–89). First, this system came with the imposition of the audit culture, whose history I have briefly explained above. Commissioners and funders required either quality marks or paper trails and spreadsheets to provide evidence of the effective use of the monies provided. The resulting framework involves marketization and bureaucratiza-tion in equal measure, with every resource ring-fenced for specific purposes. The advice sector, as a result, has come to mimic the government by imbib-ing a kind of self-imposed disciplinary regime. Second, the commissioning system has made it necessary for formerly separate and disparate organiza-tions to create what Alice Forbess and I have called "patchwork" partnerships *with* each other (Forbess & James 2017, 6–11; see also Zaloom & James 2023), sometimes successfully but often revealing irreconcilable approaches and inequalities between institutions. Third, in a seemingly paradoxical move, they have often been instrumental in pitting local advice organizations *against* each other in a scramble to make tenders for the few monies that remain.

Grouping together voluntary organizations as partners to deliver a ser-vice can be "like herding cats," said campaigner Andy Benson of the National Coalition for Independent Action. "Very often it ends in tears," he pointed out, "because you're dealing with groups of voluntary organizations who ef-fectively have been forced to work together in a situation in which they might have radically different historical origins, interests, priorities, political per-spectives, etc."[8] The sector is characterized by a diversity rather than a synergy of interests, and disparities in size and levels of professionalization among partners can make it difficult to arrange a collaboration between equals. Benson pointed out that even when such partnerships do arise, if they fail to make a winning bid they can easily be killed off by the commissioning process. In practice, bigger, more professionalized charities tend to have a closer relationship with local authorities and other funders, and this enables them to call the shots in partnerships, as the following case demonstrates.

One collaborative move was led by Simi Ryatt, of Hammersmith and Fulham Citizens Advice (CA).[9] Strapped for cash, the local authority was looking to close the library. There was a move to use the building to house a range of NGOs, all working out of one site, as a way to rationalize assets. The CA branch was offered the lease on condition that it continue to provide library services in order to comply with the terms of the lease. This development later led the way, establishing a model that was followed by CA branches more widely. However, it was not simply buildings but also new sources of funds that were needed. Seeking to find these, the CA noted that financial literacy initiatives were "where the money was," and it started projects aimed at bringing these skills to specific groups, each subsidized through a different fragment in the patchwork: Martin Lewis for ex-offenders, Comic Relief (in partnership with the local credit union) for older persons, and so on. This decentralized fund-seeking involved organizations putting much significant energy into forming alliances at the local level. While these enjoyed considerable success, Simi did question the logic of forcing the creation of partnerships for their own sake. Such expenditure of effort, she thought, might have been better spent on the actual job of giving advice. Her objection was leveled at one of the big national organizations, which was "required" as a participant in the bid, to make the alliance plausible. This bigger organization, however, had access to other sources of funds and was less firmly committed to the partnership than its smaller counterparts (its representative often failed to show up for partnership meetings). In sum, the enforcement of partnerships was serving both to incentivize novel patchworks and simultaneously to put strain on the seams that stitched these together.

The switch from grant funding to commissions that underpinned such alliances in the first place was, according to Benson, "a function of statutory funders no longer . . . [being] willing to maintain their own internal infrastructure. . . . [I]n preference they move into a procurement approach in which they effectively pass the risk of managing a community to the voluntary sector provider." Evoking something of the spirit of campaigning and advocacy that prevailed during the 1960s, he noted the contradictory way in which such de-centralized outsourcing was combined with its opposite: consolidation.

> That, coupled with the wish to simplify their own life by rolling lots of in-dividual arrangements into one contract . . . has led to the situation we're in. . . . [T]hey now say "well, instead of having 15 grants of £20,000 each, we're now going to have one contract for £225,000 . . . and then we're going to procure that." And if the organizations want to continue getting money, they're going to just have to work together and be a consortium.

Bearing out Benson's observation, the creation of partnerships in response to recurrent yet unpredictable funding possibilities has had some unintended consequences, though ones that were not necessarily unforeseeable. At one meeting we attended, an organization called Social Action for Health (SAfH) was preparing to bid for a contract for the second time and was discussing this with the commissioner from the local authority. That local authority was a partial funder of one of several partnerships that SAfH had proactively created in response to the original change from grants to commissions and contracts. The specific partnership presently seeking renewal of its funding was one of three set up by SAfH, each serving a different area in North/East London, to offer advice in doctors' rooms, drawing advisers from local com-munity fora and informal ethnic associations as well as from Law Centres and CA offices. During the course of the meeting, it became clear to SAfH's coordinating officer that some of the agencies involved in the existing part-nership were actually in the process of making *their own* separate bids for the funds—independent of that partnership and in competition with it. While the logic of free-market efficiency might suggest that the best bidder would win irrespective of the specific parties involved, it seemed clear in this case that pitting different partners against each other would entail losses of time, effort, and income. If the desired result was to keep the advice enterprise afloat, the energy expended and the frustrations undergone by those who had originally devised the funding partnership looked to be more than they were worth. Yet no alternative presented itself. The system of competitive tendering was veering toward such outcomes despite the cozy-sounding language of "partnership."

However, rather than just going through the motions to please funders, as in these cases, it has also been possible for small coalitions to spring up, developing organically between local agencies whose services complement one another. As Andy Benson said, "voluntary organizations in a local area working together strategically can be a good thing" if they can develop a common identity and interests. (As I show later in this chapter, some local authorities, in addition to funding advice agencies, actively collaborate with them.)

Overall, these strategies—whether competitive counter-bids or concerted collaborations—were attempts to respond to the changing exigencies of government funding while continuing to offer counsel to clients seeking help to manage their household budgets. In the process, by "sorting out income" for clients, they were enabling the state, at the local level, to balance its own budgets (Kirwan & James 2019). Before discussing this dual redistributive function performed by advisers, I turn to a special case: debt advice.

Fair Share or Levy?

As noted earlier, debt advice in the UK, although addressing part of the problem cluster that is inextricably linked to its other components, has a separate identity and set of funding streams. I became aware of its rather idiosyncratic character when co-writing a paper—commissioned by Black Sash—aimed at throwing light on South Africa's much smaller advice sector and understanding how debt advice is arranged and resourced elsewhere.[10]

The UK, I discovered, has divergent forms of such advice, which have long existed side by side. Following many tweaks and adjustments made by successive governments to promote greater or lesser levels of state or market involvement, and many changes of name (and acronym), these different forms continue to co-exist, but with market mechanisms increasingly prevalent. In line with the "mixed economies" mentioned earlier (Cunningham 1998), these sources of funding are: the charitable/NGO sector (including donations from companies and/or staffed by volunteer or unpaid labor), the state, and market mechanisms (through money paid in by commercial lending companies). The third of these, in turn, has two subdivisions that have co-existed since 2010. The voluntary one, known as Fair Share, began in the 1990s under the Conservative government and remained in place under the New Labour government (1997–2009), while the mandatory one, levy-funded advice, was introduced as politics swung rightwards after 2010 following the defeat of

New Labour and the establishment of a Conservative and Liberal Democrat Coalition. It was intended to make up for the shortfall when state funding was cut. The resulting hybrid combines sometimes uneasy bedfellows but continues nonetheless.

Fair Share-funded advice, which follows a kind of corporate social responsibility model, was imported to the UK from the US in 1993. It involves an agreement between creditors and debt advisers. After a debt advice encounter, a debt management plan is drawn up in which the debtor commits to monthly payments being disbursed to various creditors. To subsidize debt advice, those creditors in turn pay back a fixed percentage of the amount they now receive (as a result of the advice intervention) in debt repayments, an amount that is then given to the debt advice agency. By 1996 a majority of mainstream consumer credit firms had signed up to make these voluntary contributions (Wyman 2018). Further complex interweavings of private funding sources resulted as successive governments intensified their regulation of the sector. When the New Labour government's state-funded scheme was axed by the 2010 Coalition government, the levy-funded system was introduced in order to make up for the shortfall. The legislative basis for the levy, following several years of discussion, was the Financial Services Act of 2010, which amended the Financial Services and Markets Act of 2000: it was used to fund what eventually became the Money Advice Service (MAS). By 2012, the MAS, funded in this manner, with the levy collected by the FSA (Financial Services Authority), had been "given a statutory duty to work with partners to improve the availability, quality and consistency of debt advice across the UK."[11]

The act introducing this levy was aimed at taxing all corporations and companies (glossed as "payment institutions") that lend money via electronic, automated systems. Besides paying other statutory fees, it required each such "money issuer" to "contribute towards the cost of the Consumer Financial Education Body (CFEB)" (as MAS was then known) with a levy proportional to the size of the institution and the extent of its business.[12] By 2021 a division of labor had emerged in which the DWP (Department of Work and Pensions) determined the annual amount, the FCA (Financial Conduct Authority—as the FSA has now become) levied the financial services sector, and MaPS (Money and Pensions Service—an "arm's-length body, sponsored by the Department for Work and Pensions"[13]) controlled how the funds were spent. About £65 million of debt advice funding was available for 2020, divided equally between home finance firms (mortgages and so on) and the consumer credit industry, but an additional £38 million was later allocated in response to the COVID-19 pandemic.[14]

One of these market mechanisms has been shown to yield more reliable returns than the other (Table 4.1). The Fair Share or voluntary model ties the income of advice agencies to the amounts that commercial companies manage to recoup in repayments from those who owe them money. But when a debt adviser counsels a client and lays out a debt management plan for paying creditors in installments, additional organizations—such as the tax man, energy suppliers, mobile phone companies, and the like—will stand to benefit from the repayment of arrears, beyond those actually paying that share, as further discussed below. The levy, in contrast, decouples funding from the outcomes of any given advice encounter. The Fair Share model has been criticized as *not* entirely fair: a 2019 review of debt advice funding noted that "to the extent that debt advice assists organizations in recovering debts, they should pay for it. This is not universally the case now" (Wyman 2018, 24). The levy system is, in contrast, seen as a relatively stable source of income for debt advice.

Both systems, however, are inadequate in that they fail to acknowledge a key point made in this book: not all debt is incurred to bodies recognized as official or commercial credit providers. As noted by Bruce Carruthers and discussed in Chapter 5, debts are understood, in liberal thought, as involving a voluntaristic contract between agents operating in a free market, in which

TABLE 4.1: Fair share and levy systems

Fair Share	Levy
Voluntary	Mandatory: based on "polluter pays" idea
Introduced from US in 1993	Introduced in 2010 when state funding withdrawn
Debt advice results in debt management plan	Debt advice results in debt management plan
Debt advice agency is reimbursed from voluntary repayments to creditor	Debt advice agency is reimbursed from mandatory contributions by all electronic money issuers to state's MAS
Yields uncertain returns	Yielded £65 million in 2020, divided between home finance and consumer credit advice services

one party promises to pay back another. In situations where such contracts are lacking, such as those of arrears to the providers of services, these agencies become creditors by default (Carruthers 2022, 15). The problems suffered by those seeking advice, as already noted, tend to form "clusters" whose components are difficult—but important—to unravel. Each of these allegedly separate elements, if an advice client is in arrears, will likely require to be repaid. It is not just banks and other financial services firms, but also telecom companies and electricity and water providers, as well as statutory bodies such as local councils and HMRC (the tax office), to which such clients owe money. Even the levy system, despite yielding more stable returns, leaves the telecom providers and other institutions as incidental beneficiaries of the advice, free of any obligation to pay the levy even though they benefit from the advice. That is, they are repaid as a result of, but do not help to fund, that advice.

There is more at stake than reliability. The market-based character of debt advice funding has been criticized by debt advisers—the end users of the funding—because of the targets and conditions that accompany the levy, much like the system of audits outlined earlier in this chapter.[15] First, the funding comes with unrealistically high targets for advisers; there is an expectation that the money needs to be used not just effectively and efficiently, but in a way that every penny spent should somehow represent an investment that yields returns. Second, there is a sense of unfairness as some corporations find themselves paying via *both* schemes. "The financial services industry . . . are already directly funding some provision as part of their Corporate Social Responsibility [i.e., via Fair Share]. . . . They may stop that first funding route because . . . who wants to pay for it twice?" said one funder (IFF 2012, 119).

There is, then, the motivation to get the "best value" for the creditors paying the levy, with the implication that pushing the levy too high or not meeting the targets by delivering enough "completed" cases risks the creditors cutting down either on forbearance or on the funding they already give through Fair Share. Although the levy does not explicitly drive an expectation that each creditor will receive full repayment in the same way as does Fair Share funding, there are still creditor expectations to consider.

Perhaps cutting to the chase in a more fundamental way, some have criticized the independence of the sector. Debt advice funded by creditors—through either scheme—means that advice is part of the system, and that system is in the business of keeping people in the orbit of creditors (Davey 2017, 2022; James et al. 2021). Debt advice as implemented by the MAS was promoted as a win-win solution: one that achieves benefits for debtors *and* creditors alike (the latter, mainly big financial companies, exert continual pressure on the government to justify the levy). Debt advice funded by a market mechanism in this way, however, favors those indebted people with disposable income, and/or promotes the practice of debtors making small token payments that ultimately keep people connected to their lenders until the day when their circumstances improve. Thereafter, they will carry on borrowing (Davey 2017, 2022).

There has also been concern about the MAS itself. With the auditing, quality assurance and box-ticking increasingly ramped up; the system became more bureaucratic, establishing a triage system that meant clients only got "tailored advice" if they were identified as having a greater level of need. A potentially fairer option, suggests Ryan Davey, would be a bolder levy than the UK's current one. Funding has to be provided in such a way to meet need, irrespective of numerical targets and so-called efficiency.[16]

In contrast to this market mechanism, the funding models that seem to work best for clients, claimed one adviser,[17] are those housing associations and foundations related to specific professions. These deal with restricted groups rather than the public in general and are self- or charity-funded rather than depending on the credit industry. One example is the Charity for Civil Servants,[18] another is Perennial, the Horticulture Industry Charity.[19] Both offer debt advice to members. As well as having lower numeric targets, or lacking these altogether, these organizations are able to offer debt advisers higher pay and better working conditions.

Similarly the austerity policies have increased the public's reliance on the voluntary and charitable sector. At about the time, in 2010, when official government policy was to cut funding across the board, all advice services were hit hard. Advice offices, strapped for cash, were forced (for example in Plymouth) to see 60 percent more clients every week than before. These cuts have seen an increase in advice run by volunteers, often church-based, and aimed at the poorest and most vulnerable (Davey 2022). In this particular section of the mixed economy, then, charity-based support remains important and is indeed becoming more so.

Separate Streams: The Logic of Referral

Having outlined the separate ways in which each type of advice—for welfare and debt problems respectively—is resourced, we now turn to the process through which a client who approaches with a query relating to one aspect of the "problem cluster" is referred from one to the other. Reforms and their related audits entail the obligation to make boundaries between these, drawing in each case on the appropriate source. To ensure this, referrals are an essential part of the process. But they pose several contradictions. On the one hand, agencies are given specific targets: numbers or percentages of cases that they ought to be referring to other, more specialist agencies. SAfH was told to redirect appropriate numbers of cases to mental health charities like Mind, for example, on the grounds that they will have expertise in a particular area. Referral-based models of this kind have been seriously thought through in all their ramifications. This was evident from discussions with one informant, who favored a partnership that distributed expertise between different players:

> We were interested in striking a potential deal . . . between our organization and others. As provider of legal services, we gather basic information and present that information so you won't need to, then we make ourselves available for referrals.[20]

Such a division of labor is framed and justified by reference to effectiveness and efficiency, thought to be measurable through systems of audit. It is also linked to the conviction that most problems can, in the end, be solved: it is conceived of as part of a process through which people, once offered appropriate advice by a specialist, will either have the presenting issue dealt with or will be gradually weaned off advice, made more independent, and become more able to deal with their own problems. This resembles the aim, in South Africa, to move from "protection" to "autonomy," as outlined in Chapters 2 and 3. One borough councilor put it like this, during a meeting where she was enjoining members of a local authority-funded advice consortium to behave more rationally and transparently, in accordance with this model of self-reliance:

> We need to look at how we monitor referrals. How high the need is—are we doing the best job? We want people to be more independent. . . . Our responsibility is to make people better equipped. So—where do we refer them to?[21]

However, such rationally planned models of efficiency foundered when, as was often the case, the complexity of the case indicated that a variety of specialisms was required. Even better, someone was needed who might grasp how they all interconnect. This was acknowledged by the same adviser: "If someone has really complex issues, that is when there is a problem with referral."

An indication that "referral" is often inappropriate was the way some agencies generated resentment by referring cases onward too often. It was felt that this was sometimes done, not simply in the interests of applying the appropriate specialism, but also to "get the person off one's back." This accusation was made of some branches of an advice agency that was suspected of sending people to other agencies while including those people in their audit figures for people helped.

Referral-based models likewise proved inadequate where there was no neat mapping of supply onto demand. This often proved to be the case. At some moments, demand exceeded supply. Appointments with specialist advisers—like those concerned with housing or with debt—were often unavailable. At other moments and in other areas, however, the reverse was true. There was demand for advice, and specialists were available for consultation, but they were not getting the work, since specific pockets of money were designated to fund only those referrals made by particular advisers, or for those who lived in given areas.

Overall, the reasons for such mismatches lay in the undue parceling-off of different arenas. It was as though—unlike water that flows predictably and according to immutable laws of gravity along channels designed by engineers—"advice demand" sometimes collected in pools, and the best-laid plans of officers and funders were unable to divert it to where it might best find "advice supply."

Conjoined Streams: Frontloading Advice

Operating in sharp contrast to the logic of specialist referrals are initiatives that bring together divergent agencies in an attempt to tackle all aspects of a "problem cluster" by "frontloading advice." The background, as noted earlier, is the way central and local government follow contradictory impulses in times of austerity cuts. Funds, on which advice offices partially depend, devolve downward. But so do austerity cuts. With their central funding slashed, and being able to offer only restricted advice services, local authorities start collecting their taxes more aggressively.[22]

In the search for funds to keep advice offices afloat, many have recognized that offering (and finding funding for) welfare beneficiaries, despite austerity cuts, is the way to go. In what may appear as generosity but has an element of enlightened self-interest, several local authority-funded initiatives have continued or even augmented their personalized, face-to-face advice offering. They attempt to supplement their dwindling revenues by redirecting more central government resources into the community, in the process lessening the drain on their own resources. Alice Forbess and I gained insight into this when interviewing Paul Yates, of the law firm Freshfields Bruckhaus Deringerm. He pointed out that advice funded by local authorities practically pays for itself because, particularly in an area or city with high unemployment and under-employment, enabling local citizens to maximize their income from the central government benefits schemes that are administered by DWP and HMRC brings money into the local community and boosts local tax revenues. In addition to this, councils are obliged by law to house certain categories of vulnerable people, including families with children threatened with destitution and homelessness. Since little housing is available, councils can spend vast amounts of money on "temporary" bed and breakfast accommodations over extended periods of time. By preventing such destitution, the local authority achieves significant savings. Helping people claim all the centrally funded benefits to which they are entitled (through benefits advice), and by assisting debtors in prioritizing their debts (through debt advice), can enable local authorities to help people pay rent (often to those authorities themselves in their role as social landlord) and local tax (likewise helping to replenish their own coffers). While their help with the management of household budgeting increases local authority revenue, it also reduces the amount these authorities would be obliged by law to spend on rehousing people should they face eviction or become homeless (Forbess & James 2017) in settings of limited state housing supply.

Some such authorities, in addition to funding advice agencies, collaborate with them. "Frontloading" advice—attempting to forestall the emergence of problems down the line—is the result. Kingston Local Authority, which managed an extensive housing stock, was in 2014–15 seeking a way to deal with the rent arrears and other problems of its own (i.e., council) tenants. It was particularly concerned about the coming of the new benefit, universal credit. This would reduce its control over certain key devices—housing benefit and discretionary housing payments—that it was using to mitigate the loss of welfare benefits. It found a way to bridge the disjuncture between local and central government through the deployment of a Welfare Reform Operational Group. By bringing together the local (officers from the council, the local CA, and other charitable agencies) with the national (a representative from the DWP to provide information on the cases and claims of defaulting tenants), it bridged the gap between these two tiers of government, both offering support to vulnerable welfare beneficiaries and protecting their own bottom line.[23] Such initiatives were multi-focused: they attended to the need to help clients, while simultaneously ensuring that rent arrears did not accumulate and leave themselves, as local government, out of pocket.

Here, then, were new models that offered face-to-face advice, in a context of austerity where the overall emphasis was on cost cutting. Their protagonists were almost evangelical in their commitment to what they saw as a utopian alternative. What gave them extra clout was that they also had a pragmatic side, being concerned with fiscal sustainability.

Conclusion

Under conditions of intensified financialization twinned with austerity, the UK's advisers rely on the patchworking activities of organizations and agencies. As experts with particular specialties who assist householders in categorizing resources, they decide whether and how to partition, and assign, aspects of the problem clusters with which their clients present: to benefits, to work, or to debt. By finding ways, at a higher level, to keep their work going, and, at a face-to-face interpersonal one, to guide strapped families through entangled knots of issues, they also establish distinctions among the sources they draw together (Zaloom & James 2023).

Before proceeding to the final chapter, we can return to our comparative frame, asking whether anything might be learned from the UK case for the South African one: especially in the case of debt advice. Would a levy-funded market mechanism be feasible—one that pays to alleviate problems caused by excessive lending to householders? And would it be desirable, if so? To collect the levy imposed on creditors and redistribute it to the providers of debt advice, the UK has depended on its financial regulator, the FCA, which has a robust bureaucracy and system of audit. South Africa has appropriate institutional strength, with its Financial Sector Conduct Authority (FSCA), part of whose remit is to provide financial education programs and promote financial capability. However, there are problems of divided administration that mitigate against such a move. There is a split across various ministries and regulators, with the financial services industry falling under the National Treasury while the credit industry and consumer protection are overseen by the Department of Trade, Industry, and Competition (DTIC), of which the National Credit Regulator is part (see Chapter 2). There are also problems of regulation and enforcement. "Cash loans," payday lenders, and *mashonisas* (see Table 1.2 in Chapter 1), although nominally required by law to register with the NCR, have tended to ignore such requirements and would need to be brought into line to ensure that they operate within the law.

Beyond these institutional factors, there are larger questions about debt advice. Facilitating debt repayment, as noted above, can be seen as buttressing a legal and financial culture that advantages creditors, because it encourages low-income families to embrace and become reliant on finance while ignoring the numerous structural inequities that have led them into debt in the first place. Firsthand observations such as those in the next chapter persuade me, however, that such advice remains necessary, and is an important contributor to the public good if it can help allay individual fears and the sense of a lack of control to which the poorest debtors may sometimes—though not always, as this book argues—be subject.

FIVE

Balancing the Books
Formats and Technologies

THIS CHAPTER IS CONCERNED with the increasing use of automated systems—also called "techno-political" (von Schnitzler 2016)—to recover debts. The best-known of such systems are those that have been put in place by commercial companies, as seen earlier in the discussion of South Africa's infamous case of Net1, the grant distribution agency-cum-bank that lent to welfare beneficiaries using their payments to secure repayment in automated fashion. Lesser known are similar systems used by states. It is these and their effects on low-income people, who both work and depend on such benefits, that I analyze in this chapter.

Such systems, with their algorithmic and calculative character, might seem to be a matter for discussion more among mathematicians or economists than anthropologists. Alternatively, since they are used by government welfare agencies in the process of allocating benefits, they may be an appropriate topic for scholars of social policy and law. And indeed, such scholars have written about them, often in a deeply critical vein, given the profound effects they, backed by the full weight of the state, have on people. My approach here, however, is to see them from a perspective inspired by the anthropology of economy, particularly the work of Jane Guyer on the concept of the household and on associated processes of "conversion."

Guyer—both individually (1981) and with Pauline Peters (Guyer & Peters

1987)—set the terrain for understanding how households, seemingly discrete units separate from one another and from wider structures of power and economy, are in fact interwoven with those structures. Writing from research in Atlantic Africa, she showed how the household should be seen not as a static or bounded unit, but rather as "a group constituted according to concepts, rights, obligations" (1981, 103). Focusing on the relationships between these domestic groupings and wider processes, Guyer argued that such relations created opportunities for selection and recombination, or "areas of freedom about marriage, parenthood, residence, work, and the constraints of making a living" (1981). Despite the importance of these wider processes, anthropologists should not (indeed could not) simply switch to examining global political economic phenomena; to be faithful to our observations, she claimed, we must encompass the fact that "the relationship between micro and macro, local structures and external fields, is a dynamic one" (Guyer 1981, 104). Concepts, rights, and obligations, she argued, connect households with an external field of "extrafamilial ties," such as political and economic ones (Guyer 1981, 104; see also Zaloom & James 2023). Her later essays (2004) went further, helping us—as Caitlin Zaloom and I have noted—to conceptualize how the financial currencies of the global economy are integrally connected to householding practices of building kin and aspiring toward prosperity. Guyer, we show, provides insights into "the disjunction between institutional projections (such as those by neoclassical economists) [and] . . . stable and circumscribed domestic units and . . . practices" (Zaloom & James 2023, 403). By exploring how these disjunctions are both created and breached, and how conversions occur between them, her work "directed anthropologists to investigate the linkages among value registers, the work of engineering crossings among them, and the monetary and social profit of those gambits" (Zaloom & James 2023, 403).

But how exactly do these insights into the porous character of the household help with an understanding of algorithm-based technologies used by the state to recover debt? They do this in two ways. Firstly, they give us a grasp of the power of institutional projections and infrastructures that define the household as a discrete space, that appear to exist at a "higher" level beyond the reach of that household (see Ferguson & Gupta 2002), and that seem impervious to any appeals against its rulings that householders might make. Secondly, they help us critically interrogate the way the model of the household has been extended upwards and outwards, providing a kind of obligatory blueprint for budgeting at other levels. The belt-tightening projects undertaken by states in the name of austerity were explicitly modeled on the archetype of the frugal domestic unit in which careful budgeting must ensure that income and outgoings always match. At a workshop held in 2016 to discuss austerity, Claudio Sopranzetti pointed out that the "tightening of the belt" that austerity proposes is "discursively predicated upon a flattening of scales, directed by a master-narrative that equates national economies to households" (Sopranzetti 2016, 4): a rhetorical flourish that serves to pass down the financial burden from one "scale of governance to the next one, in a game of hot potato," creating "a trend toward the decentralization of financial costs away from the national coffers to local institutions and scales—whether regions, provinces, municipalities, families, or individuals" (2016, 4; see also James & Kirwan 2019, 682). The balancing of books that results is one that imposes state imperatives to make each of these levels pay for itself, in autonomous fashion. But householders and families at the local level often bear inordinately unequal costs, for reasons to be explained below.

Advocating such processes of frugal budgeting is pervasive in writings about debt. Previous chapters of this book have alluded to these as an important impulse that has accompanied the rapidly increasing uptake of credit around the globe. As those aspiring to better lives and upward social mobility have borrowed in greater numbers and to a greater extent, so have systems been developed of cost calculating and financial literacy. These have been seen in less than positive terms by many critics. This is particularly because, even where they may appear useful, they are more appropriate for those who have already reached, than for those who aspire towards, middle-class status (see Zaloom & James 2023, 405; and Chapter 1). Designers and advocates of such programs, however, defend them on the very obvious grounds that they help to guard against the hardship entailed in the eventual (future) repayment of extortionate amounts of interest.

These financial literacy programs are undertaken, and promoted to others, on the grounds that income and outgoings should not be unsustainably unmatched. They are designed primarily to advise those who must face up to commercial companies as creditors. But considering other kinds of attempts to "balance the books," as this chapter does, takes us into a space where state and market actors and institutions are entangled, and indeed where the state often looms *larger* as creditor than do banks or credit card companies. Such examples require us to explore, in some detail, the nature and effects of highly automated systems of payment and repayment: systems that belie any idea—or possibility—of individuals as having choice, discernment, or the need (or capacity) for financial literacy. It is in the face of such robot-like techno-political infrastructures (von Schnitzler 2016) that individuals may feel least able to act—whether as autonomous agents or as political groupings.

Being in debt to the state differs in important ways from being in debt to a commercial lender. To advance a view that might perhaps be judged overly liberal, this is because it does not involve a voluntaristic contract between agents operating in a free market, in which one party "promises" to pay back another (Carruthers 2022). Instead, it arises "without prior consent or explicit promises," in circumstances where "no lender has assessed the borrower's willingness and ability to repay." The US-based example provided by Carruthers is of "someone who fails to pay their federal income taxes," who has thus "turned the federal government into a creditor, although the government didn't agree" to this arrangement (2022, 15). The cases discussed below are similarly concerned with debts to the state, but under conditions in which it is the citizen who "didn't agree" to the arrangement and discovers only later that monies are owed. Corresponding to the lack of choice or of "free agreement," and in response to the set of automated infrastructures to which the person owing is then subjected, it is certainly here that forms of advice (if not financial literacy) have perhaps proved most valuable, even essential. Interestingly, such advice, too, involves bureaucratized and regulated structures and systems that may be subject to high-tech audits and cross-checks. Both the problem and the solution bear the imprint of rigid-seeming calculative arrangements.

The scenarios discussed in this chapter are concerned with balancing the books in different ways. One, in South Africa, is alluded to in passing while the other, in Britain, occupies center ground. In both, the logic of a system often encountered by low-income people—that of "buy now pay later," "hire purchase" (James 2015, 33, 50, 67), or "life on an instalment plan" (Torkelson 2018)—has been curiously invoked, tweaked, or reversed. In one (South Africa), householders or citizens are required to pay before the event for things they use or consume later, such as electricity. Here, no promise is involved: rather, the system is designed so as to ensure that no such promise is required, that no trust is in danger of being broken, and that the books are balanced in advance. It could be seen as a system of debt collection before the fact. In the other (the UK), as in many countries with similarly comprehensive welfare arrangements that use high-tech digital ways of reckoning finances (Millar & Whiteford 2020), the arrangement is inverted. Householders or citizens receive money in advance but, with increasing frequency, are required to repay a large sum at a later time. Again, since repayments are often secured in automated fashion by deducting them from *future* payments, debt collection poses few problems for the creditor/state. But it can leave welfare recipients in the lurch. Those who design such techno-political systems make assumptions about the nature of employment and of household composition. They are motivated by a book-balancing ideology of accountancy, taking it as axiomatic that welfare beneficiaries, if they work or alter their living arrangements, ought, by rights, to pay back. If not, money must be clawed back. Such designers are either totally ignorant of, or willfully blind about, the wildly fluctuating character of income streams for those in insecure employment. They also make assumptions about a "normal" household, unaware (or deliberately ignoring) that its members may differ from one week to the next and may no longer be in residence by the time the payments come through. All such variations, rather than being acknowledged, are made the basis for punitive sanctions.

Prepaid or Overpaid?

In the UK and South Africa, the two principal case studies in this book, the impulse to balance the books has come to the fore on multiple occasions. But this happened at different times and for somewhat dissimilar reasons. Both, however, arrived at a point where it was considered of paramount importance to make those at each level (whether municipal authorities, agencies, or indeed families) "pay for themselves."

In late apartheid South Africa, in reaction to apartheid's system of cross-subsidization by richer (white) areas of poorer (black) ones, Antina von Schnitzler describes an attempt to make each local authority fiscally responsible or autonomous.[1] This was done, not by levying taxes, but by trying to recoup "rents" (including charges for services like water, electricity, and so on). This attempt is seen by von Schnitzler as having had the effect of construing black residents as rent-paying subjects rather than citizens who pay universal taxes (2016, 80), thus avoiding solidarities that might have led to challenge or unrest. Nevertheless, this initiative *was* met by widespread protests mounted by householders against the broader, and soon to collapse, apartheid system. Indeed, these protests were likely instrumental in helping to topple that system. The subsequent advent of democracy saw the authorities, in yet further techno-political moves, install prepaid water meters. Although these might have had the effect of dissipating political action yet further, through their normalization of "fiscal citizenship" they were aimed, in theory, at preventing the build-up of householders' arrears to the state (von Schnitzler 2016, 76). I return to this case later.

In austerity Britain, post-2010, a different set of policies and pressures resulted in measures that had a somewhat similar outcome. They too resulted in an infrastructural system, in this case operating via the distribution of benefits, aimed to recoup money and to turn householders, as far as possible, into "fiscal citizens" (von Schnitzler 2016) that pay for themselves. In the process, the algorithm-based calculus was paired with austerity measures through which funds provided to local authorities dwindled, producing ever-intensifying demands for the repayment of overpaid benefits as well as increased pressure on local authorities themselves to balance the books in order to keep afloat.

But how does the process of recouping welfare overpayments operate, and how does it affirm the imposition of a model of the frugal household? Our 2014–15 research in welfare and debt advice offices in London and southern England showed the increased enforcement of this model on both these scores. To understand the first of these—the modeling of frugal self-sufficiency at the level of families and domestic groupings—we need to return briefly to Chapter 1. As noted there, the UK's social security system, before its most recent reform to produce the single universal credit benefit payment, combined a range of funds: council tax benefit, child tax credits, working tax credits, housing benefit, income support, disability living allowance (renamed personal independence payment), and job seeker's allowance (renamed employment support allowance) (see Table 1.1 in Chapter 1).

These have been administered by a variety of agencies, ranging from local authority–run departments responsible for housing, social services, and council tax collection, to national ones such as the Department of Work and Pensions (including its Jobcentre Plus and other agencies) and the tax office or inland revenue (HMRC) with its systems of tax credits (TCs). And, as noted in Chapter 1, while welfare dependent households often supplement their income from these different sources by borrowing from commercial companies or payday lenders, the debts they owe to the state have started to outstrip any arrears they may have to such private creditors. Sociolegal researcher Samuel Kirwan, using figures from the Bank of England and Citizens Advice, evidences the disproportionately intensifying problem of "debts-to-government"

(2021b, 13). This includes both people owing the local authorities, with a "striking increase in households facing arrears on Council Tax" (Kirwan 2021b, 13; Spooner 2021) and those owing money to central government departments, such as the DWP and HMRC, that have been stepping up demands for repayment from those allegedly paid too much. Alternatively, and more efficiently, the amount overpaid may simply be deducted from *future* payments—a procedure greatly facilitated by high-tech calculation and automation.

The 2013 introduction of universal credit (UC), the new benefits system bringing together—allegedly to simplify—the many means-tested benefits listed above,

> introduced a new legal framework and set of institutional practices for recovering benefits overpayments through deductions from benefits awards. This was facilitated by the expanding and enhancement of data sharing capabilities between government agencies and other information services. (Kirwan 2021b, 13–14)

This has made it possible for one department's paying too much up-front to be counterbalanced by another department's paying proportionately less in the future. In short, as large numbers of claimants moved from these so-called legacy benefits such as TC (tax credit) and HB (housing benefit) to universal credit, there were increasing numbers of "overpayment" demands (Kirwan 2021b; Schwartz & Spooner 2021) and a correspondingly greater use of automated deductions as a means of recouping these overpayments.

From the point of view of policy analysts, this has been described as a system of "pay now, establish entitlement later" (Millar & Whiteford 2020, 6), but from the point of view of those receiving such letters and demands—and those in the advice-giving fraternity who assist them—it has been regarded as a case of giving with one hand and taking away with the other.[2] The cases detailed below will give some insights into the ways in which these demands and deductions, "together with the significant squeeze upon benefits and employment income faced by low-income households," have "amplified the financial and emotional consequences that accompany it" (Kirwan 2021b, 14). Kirwan notes that "As UC has rolled out, the number of claims subject to deductions rose sharply: from one in ten claimants in May 2017 to a full third of claimants in May 2018" (2021b, 16). Among other effects, such deductions, by reducing householders' income, have caused many to turn to commercial lenders to make up the difference.

So much for the effects of the system on families. Let me anticipate the second part of my argument by recalling, from Chapter 4, a further way in which frugal householding has been imposed. Local authorities, squeezed by draconian funding cuts, and mindful both of their obligations to citizen/constituents within their areas and of the need to make *their* books balance, have responded by trying to maximize their *own* income by drawing as much as possible from the coffers of that central government (Forbess 2022, 46–47; Forbess & James 2014, 2017). They have done this, in part, by providing some resources to fund the provision of benefits advice. Using the income drawn down from the centralized benefits system, efforts can be made to help the client repay whatever debts she has—especially those "priority debts" owed to the local authority itself (James & Kirwan 2019). This approach serves both to help and support the recipient of welfare benefits and to ensure that rent arrears do not accumulate and leave the council out of pocket. The client, in conversation with and guided by the adviser, becomes, in effect, a conduit for these redistributive processes (James 2022a, 12).

Overpayments and Advice: The View from the Family

Several scholars have laid out with admirable clarity the intricate and complex workings, and effects, of the overpayments system. I return to consider these below, but my aim here is, first, to give an idea of how demands for the return of these overpayments appear from the point of view of those receiving them. These I and my fellow researchers have been able to observe through the methodological device of the "advice encounter," in which families seeking help about benefits claims interact with those who offer them counsel (James & Kirwan 2019, 673). I start by giving some excerpts from the field diary of Alice Forbess who, as a researcher on a project that explored advice in a variety of institutional settings in London and Portsmouth—an NHS hospital, a local council office, and a range of NGOs including Citizens Advice offices, Law Centres, and a charity providing a more holistic range of services (Forbess 2022, 45)—was observing some of these encounters.

In the four excerpts below, demand for the repayment of overpaid benefits feature alongside a complex mélange of other kinds of income, including wages and benefits. They show the systematic use of such demands, yet also demonstrate that the recipients of such demands often experience them as random and difficult to untangle. It is this complexity that initially spurred them to seek advice in order to unravel and understand if (and what) they owed. The fieldwork was done in 2014, just one year after the 2013 introduction of universal credit: in subsequent years, demands for benefits reclaim have become far more insistent (Kirwan 2021b). Nevertheless, these notes give insight into some of the enduring features of overpayments demands and into the hurly-burly of the debt advisers' world. These are explored here under separate headings.

Change of Circumstances: Change of Income

This case of a forty-something Newham woman advised by Will (see Box 5.1) shows the disruption caused by a "change of circumstances" (here, in hours worked). A recipient of disability benefits—the disability living allowance (DLA)—this woman had already, at various points, considered trying to work from home. But doing so would have required a constant effort to report her earnings, so that her benefits could be adjusted accordingly. Even when such changes are reported in a timely manner and readjustments are made immediately rather than building up to form huge arrears, recurrent changes in one's income can be unsettling. Given that she wished for security and wanted to be able to budget in light of her meager income, she judged it better not to introduce any sudden alterations. Her benefits were providing only just enough to survive on, but they were predictable, and a fluctuating income would have upset this balance. Her frugal attitude is evident in her wish to use the inheritance she received, straight away, in order to pay back the debts to the state that had resulted from her being "overpaid." But doing so, evidencing a sudden upswing in her income, would likely suspend her benefits, bringing yet further sources of insecurity and uncertainty about how to allocate scarce funds.

The UK, like many other countries, uses tax credits as a means of incentivizing people to work while also reducing the risk of in-work poverty (Hills 2015, 2; Millar & Whiteford 2020). These provisions are a recognition of the point made in Chapter 1: that welfare and wages often co-exist. Social protection systems that acknowledge this co-existence "put benefits alongside earnings, creating an 'income package' made up of different components and combinations" (Millar & Whiteford 2020, 4). However, observe Jane Millar and Peter Whiteford, "when income-tested provisions are in the mix, as they often are, this can create complex design and delivery problems" (Millar & Whiteford 2020, 4). One of these problems relates to timing and sequencing. As noted in Chapter 2—in the South African case—certain flows of income,

---

BOX 5.1: 2014 field diary excerpt 1

10TH APRIL 2014

Portsmouth. Will is giving advice to a 40-ish lady who wants to know how an inheritance of about £30,000 from her father will affect her benefits. She has overpayments to repay and a mortgage. She is on DLA (Disability Living Allowance) and is a carer for 18-year-old son with diabetes. She tells me: "I often thought whether I can work from home but with a fixed amount coming in it's just more practical to stay on benefits because you know what you've got coming and can budget." She talks to me about her struggle. She has no overdraft. "So painful. It will be great to have a bit of basic security." It's all about micro-budgeting in their household. Will calculates her benefits using an online calculator. She will have to use the inherited money to pay her mortgage, but once her savings drop to £16,000 she will get all her benefits back. She'd like to pay off the overpaid amount but may lose her benefits if she repays a large lump sum, says Will.

---

in and out, have a temporal regularity and can be correspondingly planned for. Mpho borrowed regularly from a formal lender in response to predictable seasonal changes that required the purchase of new clothes for her children. Others, however, are unforeseen and are pinned to urgent needs that occur out of any chronological order, requiring loans from other informal sources.

The difficulty of mapping these rapid temporal changes in need and income, in the UK case, has been recognized in government circles. Members of the House of Commons Treasury Select Committee noted that the "whole year approach" of the tax credits system is mismatched with the financial needs of the families concerned: "the monthly assessment in Universal Credit is arguably too short and the whole month approach too rigid, yet at the same time the system is too responsive to what might be short-term changes." The government was said to have underestimated the "sheer volume of changes of circumstance in people's lives," but it was also pointed out that there would be risks in being *too* responsive to such changes (Millar & Whiteford 2020, 9).

Exemplifying this point is a quote from the 2006 Hansard in the House of Lords:

[If] you seek to track every change and every three to four weeks change the credit for half the population claiming tax credits, even if the computer could handle it, I doubt very much whether the lone parent could. Such adjustments would be made six weeks in arrears and there would be no way in which that parent would be able to construct a family budget with such unreliable and non-robust flows of income, especially as some of the changes in circumstance cancel each other out. (cited in Millar &Whiteford 2020, 10)

Even if such fine-grained modifications were made, changes in employment and family structure are rarely permanent. A family might

seem eligible in some periods but not in others, when the family's needs have not fundamentally changed. . . . Most churning is related to changes in residence, employment, and household composition, and many of those changes are short-lived. (Romich & Hill 2017, quoted in Millar & Whiteford 2020, 16)

The Newham case shows how, while imposing the model of the careful book-balancing manager on the one hand, the overpayments system simultaneously undermines it on the other. The system of welfare distribution depends on authorities being up to date on the income of households, but given that many people's circumstances are complex and fluctuating, informing them requires close attention and scrupulous recordkeeping. When HMRC, DWP, or the local authority discovers it has not been informed of a change in employment or personal circumstances (or when it has been told but has erroneously failed to act on the information), overpayment demands—often for thousands, even tens of thousands of pounds—are issued.

Change of Circumstances: Single or Joint Claims

The case of Donna from Portsmouth (see Box 5.2) further demonstrates the conundrum of changed circumstances. It illustrates the theme of perhaps greatest significance for overpayment demands, which is the role they play in enforcing and structuring the composition of families and, in particular, passing judgment on the cohabitation of men and women (see Forbess & James 2014, 82). Social security payments are intended to "stabilise household incomes, both in macro-economic terms when there are recessions, or more narrowly when individuals or families experience personal, but common, risks" (Barr 1987, cited by Millar & Whiteford 2020, 3). But family circumstances may shift, especially when couples, in particular those with children, alternate between cohabiting and living apart.

> **BOX 5.2:** 2014 field diary excerpt 2
>
> **25TH APRIL 2014**
>
> Portsmouth. Donna, following a relationship breakdown, suffered from
> severe depression and anxiety, and couldn't cope. Ex stayed at her house
> part time to help look after her children, whilst living with his grand-
> mother. DWP considered he was still living with her as he was using that
> postal address, and issued a series of overpayments demands to her: £20,000
> in Housing Benefit (which she was repaying in amounts of £10 per month),
> £4,000 in Income Support, and £500 in Council Tax (also being repaid at a
> rate of £10 per week). She has been making these payments from her current
> benefits income (ESA, Child Tax Credit, Child Benefit). This could have
> been fought, Moira says. Ex was abusive and basically stalking her. DWP
> did not have a strong enough case to go to court and prosecute her. But it's
> too late to challenge it now. Donna has also applied for DLA (Disability
> Living Allowance): she is due to go up in front of ATOS in two weeks' time
> for them to assess the merits of her case.

Kirwan observes that family circumstances often shift when couples, in
particular those with children, have malleable cohabitation patterns. Col-
lectively dubbed "living together" or "undeclared partner" cases, judgments
about these affect women disproportionately. Since it is thought to be unlikely
that the presence of a husband or partner might be unintentionally misreported (Kirwan 2022, 19), the authorities automatically characterize such
cases as fraudulent. In addition to demanding their money back or automatically deducting it, they might even take claimants to court. In Donna's case,
she had been in an abusive relationship from which it was difficult to extricate
herself, given that there was childcare to be arranged, and she was relying
on her partner's help for that. Although her partner was now living with his
grandmother, he stayed in the flat on some occasions. In cases like Donna's,
the "single claimant," it is assumed, ought to be part of a joint claim—together
with the partner with whom she is reckoned to be "living together as a married couple" (Kirwan 2022, 23). The authorities found out, deemed her to have
misreported the true composition of the household, and calculated that she
had been "overpaid" a total of £24,500. The fact that she had received helpful
professional guidance in structuring these repayments—in small (though for

her barely affordable) amounts—was evidence of the value of advice in such circumstances.[3]

In deliberating about such "fraud," Kirwan explains, there is a tendency to compress complex household realities into a rigid structure of binary categories, passing a verdict on whether either "finance" or "intimacy" is prevalent. Thus are the living arrangements of couples—who might be in the process of parting, reconciling, or constructing arrangements of what Viviane Zelizer calls "differentiated ties" to manage informally the intertwined worlds of finance and intimacy (2000, 842)—represented as either "fraudulent" (motivated by an underhand desire to cheat the taxpayer) or "genuinely loving" (bereft of narrowly pecuniary considerations).

Donna's case shows how inadequate such a characterization can be. Although households may be represented in such courts as based on intimate domesticity alone, they are, as Guyer noted, co-extensive and intricately entangled, with seemingly external economic realities (1981). Householders produce adjacencies, by drawing the boundary around kin groupings or dissolving these, as the need dictates. Drawing the circle of economic obligation is a matter of moving some into and others out of kin relations in "day-by-day negotiation," as anthropologist Chris Gregory observes (2009, 152). Likewise, "widely varied relations and responsibilities that stretch across residences and generations" can be called on, and depended upon (Zaloom 2017; see also Zaloom & James 2023, 406).

Change of Circumstances: Present or Absent Children, Transnational Families

A further cause for overpayment demands is the fact that children who reach the age of eighteen are deemed to be "non-dependent," or that those who depart to live abroad with relatives are no longer officially included as family members. The Newham case of Miranda (see Box 5.3) involves a mother's adult children in fluctuating wage-earning arrangements. One starts earning a salary while another ceases to do so. Miranda receives a demand for £2,000, "overpaid" on her housing benefit, because of failing to inform the authorities of this change. In her case, the adviser points out, things are quite clearcut: the letter is "valid"; he suggests, somewhat bluntly, that the client ask her working daughter to help pay back the amount.

I switch here to some cases from my own fieldwork. In one case I observed, Maddie, a CA officer, called a client back. She told me, "He has had a letter asking for money back" because of a housing benefit overpayment of £7,000.

BOX 5.3: 2014 field diary excerpt 3

20TH OCTOBER 2014

Newham, London. Woman in her 40s called Miranda. It concerns over-payment demands. She has two kids and is 25 years old, Ecuadorian. Her benefits were suspended because she didn't inform the authorities about changes in her circumstances—she changed her place of work, and her daughter started to work whilst her son stopped working.

LT: How much did they ask you to pay?

M: About £2,000. My boss didn't find the P45 in the system. I had to get a statement from the bank showing my wages. Also they assumed my son was helping out with rent.

LT: But they were right to assume that because you didn't tell them anything. . . . It's up to you to ask your daughter to pay you. You can appeal this if you think the decision was wrong. But the notice looks valid to me.

Although employed, he qualified for this benefit in light of his low earnings. The overpayment demand, however, had been made because he failed to declare that the two children living in the household were non-dependent. Maddie discovered that the father was away in Qatar. She conferred with his adult daughter, who maintained that her father had a letter proving that he did make such a declaration. Maddie asked when the father was due back in the UK. "He needs to ask [the authorities] for an explanation as to why he owes this money. Does the letter say that? Does he have proof of the letter that he wrote back to them? Did he get a receipt for it? It might be official error." It turned out that he was due to return in a few days, and still had a week's grace. She advised that he call again, or alternatively be referred to the National Debt Line.

Here, as elsewhere, the adviser's role—assisting in the householding practices of managing income and balancing budgets—is primarily one of care. But Maddie may also need to intervene in those relationships. Informing the family of the legal status (for benefits) of non-dependents holds an important correlative: such non-dependent children must contribute financially to the household.[4] The encounter also shows that the outcome of claimants' cases hinges on

their having secured, and kept, proof. If, as claimed, this client had informed
the agency administering the housing benefit of his change in circumstances,
he would be in a stronger position to challenge the overpayment demand.
However, in the case of the housing benefit, even where an overpayment is the
result of an official error, overpayments remain recoverable by the state unless
"the claimant could not reasonably have been expected to have realized that
an overpayment was occurring," a case that is difficult to make when there are
large sums involved. The system, by putting the onus on claimants to report
their circumstances, involves punitive back-loading rather than checking
people's eligibility in advance (James & Kirwan 2019).

In yet another case, Kojo, a married Ghanaian with four children, *had*
failed to inform the authorities of changed circumstances. The worst-case
scenario—of prosecution and a court case—was avoided, however, most likely
because the "change" did not concern a couple whose conjugal cohabitation
was in question but rather a failure to report that children had been absent
from the household for a period of time. This was due to the transnational
character of the household. Kojo was a resident locally and earned £700 per
month. He sought help from CA about a demand from the tax office, HMRC,
to return child tax credit that had been overpaid. "They say I owe £14,000," he
said, pointing out that he had no other debts. The family was also in receipt
of two other forms of state welfare: housing benefits and council tax support
(not uniformly available, the latter has since been withdrawn in some areas—
see Table 1.1 in Chapter 1). His wife, who previously had a job, was currently
out of work. During her former period of employment, they found that their
oldest child "was not responding at school" and decided to send three of their
children to Ghana where they would stay with relatives and go to school. Kojo
said that he informed the school about their decision to send the children
back, but "it was my mistake not to tell the tax people," so the family continued
to receive the child benefit for all four children. The adviser, Stephen, said,
"So you owe them money? That is your debt." "You have to pay back—or go
bankrupt. But if you do, you will not get credit again. . . . It is a big sum of
money that you owe—that is the problem." Kojo affirmed that he was willing
to make repayments and was referred to Stepchange, a debt charity offering
phone-based specialist advice and non-fee-paying debt management plans.
"You pay what you can afford," Stephen told him. "The company is free—
they will help you do this." The overpaid beneficiary was here being advised
of his obligation to repay and then referred to a free (that is, levy-funded)

debt advice organization in order to reach an agreement on how this would be accomplished (James & Kirwan 2019, 9–10).

It is not only the precise details of who is living in a dwelling at any particular time that is at issue here. Families with overseas connections, some members of which may be abroad at any given time, also pose a puzzle and invite demands for the repayment of benefits awards. The model of the household on which such demands are premised is that of a fixed domestic unit with a stable set of residents, yet this belies the reality of families whose living circumstances extend across national boundaries. While depending on certain benefit payments in the UK, its members send remittances away, travel abroad to care for relatives who rely on them, or remain responsible for children living elsewhere. Earning insecure, low, or hourly wages, they may appear as state dependents in one register. But they are the ones who are depended upon in another: by the state for the taxes they pay and by the economy for the contributions that they or family members make, whether in Britain (Atfield et al. 2007) or in far-flung parts of the globe (Datta 2012; and see James & Kirwan 2019).

A decade after the fieldwork cited in these cases, it became clear that havoc was still being wreaked on families by the automation of overpayment calculations. In 2024, the press carried stories of family members "looking after disabled, frail, or ill relatives," who were receiving a benefit from DWP not previously mentioned in this book: the "carer's allowance." "Tens of thousands of unpaid carers," *The Guardian* reported, "are being forced to repay huge sums to the government and threatened with criminal prosecution after unwittingly breaching earnings rules by just a few pounds a week." As with similar cases noted in Chapter 1 and further analyzed below, these people were both receiving government benefits in recognition of their care work and working part-time. At the point where the fine balance between wages and welfare was deemed to have tipped—where they had "earned too much"— they were judged in retrospect to have become ineligible for any of the carer's allowance they had received and were sent a bill for the full sum "in some cases for more than £20,000."[5] Later that year, the Liberal Democrat leader noted the fiscal illogic of the situation. By undertaking to look after relatives on a semi-voluntary basis rather than making them a burden on the state, "family carers save the tax payer £162 billion a year," he pointed out, noting that if this anomaly were to be sorted out "many could go back into work."[6]

Overpayments and Advice: The Local Authority as Budgeting Unit

Switching to a somewhat different register, the final case (see Box 5.4) illuminates the invaluable help that consulting an adviser can bring to householders faced with apparently contradictory claims and demands. It also demonstrates how the local authority, by funding advice, tries to ensure its own fiscal self-sufficiency. The bewilderment summed up by the clients' statement "So many letters, it's confusing" is mitigated by the counsel they received: to write and seek clarification and request an appeal. The household was both being credited with extra benefits of £2,100 but also having these withheld because of overpayments of £1,100 from a different source in the complex array of benefits. Someone in the household was in receipt of ESA (employment support allowance) from DWP, which owed them the extra amount, but—as far as the adviser could make out—WTC (working tax credits) from HMRC were reckoned to have been overpaid (see Table 1.1 in Chapter 1). The adviser's recommendation that they write a letter to seek clarification, and to request a "mandatory reconsideration" of the case,[7] illustrates how advisers, even if themselves unable to untangle the "confusing" character of missives from the various benefits agencies, can empower people to take action and to seek a second hearing in the face of the random—and quite possibly incorrect—forces of bureaucracy.

This case, like many other similar ones, is an illustration of the role played by free advice in advising those beset by problems with benefits. The adviser, in a manner outlined in Chapter 4, was parsing out the kinds of advice required. The clients, in debt to the state rather than to a private company, were experiencing confusion, faced with demands for entangled sums of monies owed with elements that were difficult to separate. The adviser was sifting through a complex array of benefits, taxes, and rents, rendering some of these (from the householder's point of view) as a means to fund or subsidize the others—as seen in the case of Donna from Portsmouth who was making repayments to the council from her other benefits. Such counsel is particularly helpful in the face of those increasingly automated systems that transform welfare recipients into debtors to the state through the overpayment system of "pay now, reconcile later" (Millar & Whiteford 2020, 15).

Seen from the point of view of the local authority, however, balancing the books involves positioning itself on both sides of the ledger book, "being both a primary creditor and collector of income (in the form of Council Tax, as

---

BOX 5.4: 2014 field diary excerpt 4

16TH APRIL 2014

Newham, London. LT is doing triage/advice. She takes seven cases, including one Mandatory Reconsideration concerning an overpayment demand. (It's a bit of a mess: DWP claims both that they owe the person money and that the person owes them money).
[The couple shows her some Jobcentre Plus letters.]

LT: Why would there be an overpayment of arrears? That means they owe you £2100, so if the overpayment is £1100 and they say they owe you this, then why do they think you owe them?

They: So many letters, it's confusing.

LT: What you're having to have to do is write to them explaining this. [They give her another letter.] Yes, so this is what they're saying they owe you. [Reads from letter.] "This payment has not been sent or credited to you because we are holding details of a possible overpay-ment." Why do they owe you money in the first place?

They: We don't know.

LT: Right, what you need to do is ask for this— [underlines something in letter]. Ask why they owe you money in the first place. . . . Show me that letter again. This is June last year. . . . Other income for the household was £89, what was that? Working Tax Credit? Just put copies of that in there. Ask for Mandatory Reconsideration. When they send the decision and you're not happy with it come back to us with all the paperwork. What was the credit for and what is the over-payment? It's standard that they took Working Tax Credit off. So you need to write a letter asking, why do we owe you money and why do you owe us? [Repeats instructions.] Don't worry about that, they'll go on for years asking for the money. You just have to give the story as is. Why is there £2100 credit? Is it ESA? [Writes the woman a note as to what to put in the letter.]

---

a social landlord and as administering agency for Housing Benefit) and the principal funder of advice itself" (James & Kirwan 2019, 682). Those running and staffing advice services were playing an ambivalent role in giving counsel to people on how to balance the books. They were both incorporating and also partially resisting the belt-tightening ideology of the austerity regime, with its central government-imposed top-down high-tech initiatives. As noted in Chapter 4, their use of funds from the local authority to pay for advice services meant yielding a crop of returns from centrally funded sources. Informed by a conviction that advice practically "pays for itself" (James & Forbess 2017), they were enabling local citizens to maximize their income from central government benefits schemes and thereby boosting much-needed council tax revenues (James & Kirwan 2019, 8). Much of the counsel that advisers offered, then, "was designed to help people honour . . . commitments while challenging debts they had incurred from the incorrect award—and reclaim—of benefits" (James & Forbess 2017, 20). In the face of austerity cuts, welfare beneficiaries had become conduits through which payments from central government were channeled and diverted to replenish local authority coffers.

The husbandry involved—for families (many of them transnational), local government, and the advice charities it funds—has effects that, although often punitive, are less uniformly hegemonic than often supposed by accounts of austerity. Exploring advice encounters shows how owing money does not simply transform the identity of the beneficiary, or indeed the local authority, to render them as nothing more than debt repayors forced into humiliating acts of fiscal accountability (Adkins 2017; Forbess 2022) or fiscal citizenship (von Schnitzler 2016). Juggling various obligations, both families and the local state endeavor to meet some obligations while legitimately avoiding others. Advisers, positioned between potential sources of income and the demands and powers of the state, help to enable this balancing act. Their activities can serve the ends of redistribution and fairness rather than simply, without due consideration, implying an insistence on paying back what is owed.

Tackling High-Tech Systems Globally

The two case studies under discussion in this book—South Africa and the UK—are specific instances of a wider phenomenon. Both embody attempts to engender *fiscal citizenship*. For example, the technology used in prepaid meters, a development of the penny-in-the-slot meter used in late nineteenth-century London (von Schnitzler 2013) was then trialed in South Africa and, according to von Schnitzler, thereafter rolled out globally.[8] As if by way of proof, prepaid electricity meters in the UK were, in 2023, being "foisted on distressed customers, including vulnerable households."[9] According to think-tank Humane Energy, warrants issued without due diligence by magistrates were allowing landlords to install such meters in rental premises. The prepay system was more costly for users than the direct-debit system it replaced, and its technology enabled a daily charge simply for providing the possibility of connection, even when tenants did not buy electricity in advance. As soon as a tenant *did* make such a prepaid purchase, the electricity providers were using this as a means to automatically collect the back-dated amounts owed in daily charges. The system was enabling providers "to pick their pockets, with up to 50% of each payment swiped as clawback for arrears," thus "depriving vulnerable customers of intended protections".[10] Complicating the characterization of citizenship, here it was private landlords using systems of state enforcement to enable the collection of debts owed to private electricity companies.

Contesting the implicit claim that fiscal accountability must routinely be deprecated, however, we might consider the negative effects of neglecting it completely. It might be assumed from the material presented above that requiring poor householders to balance their own books is an unfair, even unsustainable approach. In the South African case it has been argued, however, that there are dangers in bypassing such requirements if no feasible arrangements—for example, cross-subsidization—are put in place. This was highlighted by a scientific advisory group, Sage. Decades after the installation of prepaid meters in some areas, thousands of municipalities proved to be deep in debt. The imminent collapse of water treatment and provision, which had led to a cholera outbreak, was said to be due—in settings where prepaid meters had *not* been installed—to the failure of these authorities to collect payments. A subcommittee "recommended a comprehensive series of actions, including putting the brakes on shoddy billing systems and debt collection" by municipalities that were "fuelling runaway debt to water boards"—in turn contributing to systemic failures and dysfunction in wastewater facilities. The advisory group endorsed proposals "to introduce standardized credit control and debt recovery measures across all water boards and water trading entities,"[11] because of the long-term effects on public health.

In general, however, many policy analysts agree that it is misguided to deploy "overpayment" or "pay now, settle later" systems to enforce fiscal self-sufficiency among vulnerable populations. Nonetheless, such systems are widely used, especially in countries with comprehensive welfare arrangements that use high-tech digital ways of reckoning finances (Millar & Whiteford 2020). In the US, overpayments to working people in receipt of disability benefits turned out to be associated with "low levels of education and relatively low monthly benefit amounts" (Hoffman et al. 2019): it was recommended that better communication "might help beneficiaries comply" with the requirements to report their income accurately and avoid overpayments that resulted in large debts to the state.

More critical, and less aligned with the presumption that working people ought to be obliged to keep correct records, are accounts of Australia's system of debt recovery dubbed "online compliance intervention" (OCI). This system, once again, concerns debts owed to the state, for social security overpayments, by those of working age (Carney Ao 2018, 6; Millar & Whiteford 2020). Using automated calculations, OCI was "projected to recover $2.1 billion over four years" (Carney Ao 2018). In what became known as the Robodebt scandal, the system turned out to have used statistical averages for income over sometimes lengthy periods of time. This use of averages, especially for those on hourly-paid contracts who are most likely also to be welfare beneficiaries, obscured the highly variable "true underlying patterns." The Department of Human Services, known as Centrelink, put the onus on beneficiaries to "disprove the possible overpayment" by producing or obtaining copies of pay slips" (Carney Ao 2018, 2). Its effect on those beneficiaries could have been predicted:

> [W]hen confronted with suggestions of having an overpayment, often from up to seven years ago, the least literate, least powerful, and most vulnerable alleged debtors will simply throw up their hands, assume Centrelink knows that there really is a debt, and seek to pay it off as quickly as possible. Alleged debtors do so even though the Ombudsman's report demonstrated that most debts calculated this way were greatly inflated, and that some were false (zero debts). (Carney Ao 2018, 3)

These examples expose the fundamental shortcomings of fiscal accountability when used inappropriately. They question the use of high-tech algorithmic systems to impose such accountability—such "balancing of the books"—on those who might feel themselves to be at the sharp end of these calculative processes rather than being able to use them to their own advantage. By bringing down the full weight of the state and its immovability on the heads of those with least ability to withstand it, they appear perhaps even less forgiving than do private financial companies. The frugality, and autonomy, of apparently circumscribed domestic units is thus exposed as a myth at best, a cruel joke at worst.

Conclusion

If we recall Guyer's point that "the relationship between micro and macro, local structures and external fields" as a dynamic one, and recognize that householding connects domestic groupings with an external field of "extrafamilial ties" (Guyer 1981), we might think rather differently about the situations discussed in this chapter. Such a view opens up for investigation, rather than prejudging, the particular link between households and the financial instruments that they use or to whose technical systems they are subjected. Family members, as seen in Caitlin Zaloom's book on student debt, are unlikely to achieve true self-sufficiency. Instead, they recognize that "independence must be cultivated under conditions not only of intimate connection but also of extended financial assistance." Rather than independent book-balancing, this is "enmeshed autonomy" (Zaloom 2019, 95). In a similar vein, Sohini Kar uses the term "enfolding" to describe how debtors are embroiled in both domestic relationships and the calculative abstractions that borrowing brings with it (Kar 2013). The relationship between families and finance involves "everyday mediations and translations" (Schuster & Kar 2021), "conversions" (Guyer 2004), and what Zelizer calls "relational work" (2012).

In the cases explored in this chapter, it is advisers, interacting with welfare beneficiary families, who do the "relational work" that is necessary to make overpayment demands intelligible. They help to disentangle those demands made in error from those (within the flawed logic of the "settle later" system) that are deemed legitimately payable. It is in this way that "benefits," following due scrutiny and cross-checking, become "debts," and that a matter for the "benefits adviser" can be referred sideways to a "debt adviser," paid for by a different funding stream. Transferring those cases of monies judged to be owed to the state in this way reconfigures the benefits-receiving household as a debtor. But, by offering a schedule of affordable and temporally staggered payments, advisers also help to mitigate the most egregious effects of sudden, overwhelming demands, transforming these into items of which a frugal budgeter can, in the end, make a calculative reckoning.

CONCLUSION

THIS BOOK ANALYSES MANY small-scale instances of the redistributive encounter in two different national contexts: one from the Global North (austerity Britain) and the other from the Global South (post-democracy South Africa). It has illustrated both commonalities and contrasts between them, also showing how each has changed over time. Given that the focus is shifting to reallocative processes beyond those that were tried and tested in the heyday of the welfare state, it asks how, under these circumstances, people make a living and pay for what they need and want. The shrinking of welfare in northern settings and its new instantiation via the provision of cash transfers in southern ones have seen those at the bottom of the pile—be they the unemployed, low-paid workers, or formerly middle-class people migrating to work abroad and now on zero-hours contracts—brought into the ambit of, or "enfolded within," formal financialized arrangements (Kar 2018). But the book contests the view that financialized technologies used by large-scale institutions—such as banks or governments—have hegemonic control over householders. It also repudiates the claim that wage labor is no longer a factor in shaping lives. And it complicates insights into the role played by welfare payments. The book, in sum, documents how people—those practicing self-help or seeking assistance from advisers, and those aided by court judgments that challenge illicit deductions from wages or even by the social responsibility activities of financial companies—contest demands deemed to be unjust through redistributive activities that enable clawing back.

In both settings, the need to maintain or support sustainable household-ing in the face of mounting challenges is a key factor. In the UK, as in Europe more broadly (Narotzky 2020), austerity policies mean that government agencies are withdrawing what, in the heyday of the welfare state, was more generously publicly funded and seen as a right. People are encouraged to turn to increasingly precarious casual employment rather than relying on benefits, while also being pushed to practice frugality and to economize. Advisers alternately enforce and contrive to undermine these agendas. Here, "clawing back" means maximizing income from dwindling sources and challenging repayment obligations. In South Africa, a recent democratic transition combined with financial liberalization has seen growing unemployment (though not the complete absence of wage work) and the roll-out of cash transfers. The result has been a borrowing boom. Both NGOs and private/corporate initiatives have stepped in where the state is reluctant to go, functioning to curb the otherwise untrammeled activities of lenders. Here, "clawing back" means seeking to reclaim appropriated funds while working tirelessly to challenge, in court if necessary, those who ransack pay packets and bank accounts.

The book recounts these topics by giving an account of a series of interactions at the local level—what we might, borrowing from Norman Long (2001), call the "redistributive interface." This seems to suggest something piecemeal rather than weighty or substantial. It might also, in its insistence on the importance of individual actions in small offices and local settings, be seen as going against more radical views that advocate for group action as a way of hitting back against the power of capitalism. Rather than endorsing the spirit of a utopian-sounding mobilization of the poor and vulnerable—some vision of a commons opposed to, or out of reach of, the profiteering of big business—it could be seen as focusing too much on fragments of disconnected experience, perhaps even as apolitical. I maintain, however, that there is value in exploring the significance of such close encounters, often between protagonists from seemingly separated backgrounds.

Such an approach is not, of course, a new or original one. Adopting a perspective that is broadly informed by Weber's "methodological individualism" and, in turn, by Geertz's work on economic life in his books *Peddlers and Princes* (1968) and *Sūq* (1979, reissued in 2023), I have used the extended case method to draw broader inferences from instances of ethnography. Authors who had an early association with the Manchester school—such as Freddy Bailey, John and Jean Comaroff, Bruce Kapferer, and Victor Turner—long ago noted the importance of negotiation, strategic manipulation of contradiction, and the like. Those associated with that school who took such observations forward into an exploration of development programs, such as Norman Long and Jean-Pierre Olivier de Sardan, have explored "pragmatic and interactionist" behavior (Olivier de Sardan 2015) and used an "actor centred" perspective to investigate how the "gap"—or "interface" (Long 2001)—between outside actors and the recipients of their actions can be bridged, but also what misunderstandings might remain or be newly generated.

Taking such insights on board, I have tried to show how individual actors of various kinds *create* the redistributive encounter. Of the three types of resource discussed in this book, none provides a simple and straightforward income stream. Wages may be attached by creditors,. Debts owed to creditors may be used to pay for other obligations. Welfare payments are usually not simply or straightforwardly delivered in a single neat sum. In South Africa, creditors take their cut from these; while in the UK, despite the government's welfare reform aimed at removing complexities, an understanding of one's benefits—and a challenge to the automated reduction of these—requires spreadsheets and calculus, with "income" and "outgoings" mapped against each other. Advice helps to separate complex mixtures into separate strands, at the same time effecting redistribution by helping to move funds from central to local government.

Perspectivism, Context?

A colleague who works in the natural sciences recently challenged me, asking "Don't you people in the humanities and social sciences ever come up with universal statements: laws of general application?" After thinking about it for a while, my answer to him was, "There is no law other than that there is no law." Put differently, "everything depends on the context." Insights into the contingent and relativist character of social life, with roots in Weber's interpretivist frameworks and the subdiscipline of historical sociology that resulted, have since become almost ubiquitous in anthropology. In their strongest and most recent formulation, this culturalist approach has been manifest in the theoretical insights of "perspectivism" coined by Eduardo Viveiros de Castro in Brazil—"the radically different way in which many indigenous Amerindians appear to view the world" (Killick 2014)—associated with the "ontological turn" in British anthropology of the mid-2010s. In a review article, Evan

Killick shows how, while he finds much to admire in this approach with its favoring of "radical alterity," it does have the danger

> both of overinterpreting, or perhaps over-intellectualising, alternative views and practices while also eclipsing a fuller and wider sense of the power of anthropological study itself. For me, anthropology's strength lies precisely in its ability to find, describe and discuss both similarity and difference. (2014)

The extent to which people see their actions as intelligible within some broader framework or, instead, experience their circumstances as uniquely different from those of others, is related to this point about similarity and difference. It also speaks to the wider issue of comparison that has been an implicit topic of this book. A connected point arises when one asks whether any course of action may appear intelligible, depending on whose values or whose analysis of circumstances are involved. I name two South African examples from this volume. Do the strategies followed by a woman who takes out a high-interest loan from a lender only to pay her debts to a savings club, or a woman who declines to have money on hand in case relatives whittle it away, preferring instead to approach a lender when she needs cash, make sense? Are these strategies one-off forms of action, uninformed by a broader vision of economic rationality? If so, are they best seen in terms of notions of cultural relativism: of the radical alterity and difference of alternative worldviews, as some anthropologists analyzing economic action might see things? Or are they informed by more pluralist, hybrid values, in which the mores of African communal sociability mingle with virtues such as dignity, freedom, and autonomy, which have gained greater traction in the post-apartheid environment, as well as with canny strategizing about the use of cash?

The mention of autonomy here has echoes in various parts of the book. The two examples mentioned above—of women living in somewhat marginal settings and reliant on their own savvy to deal with economic demands from lenders, relatives, and club members—recall research published two decades ago, in *Lilies of the Field: Marginal People Who Live for the Moment* (1999), edited by Sophie Day and others. As analyzed by the authors, their research interlocutors—who range from gypsy communities to London sex workers— are resistant to any attempt to characterize them as "dependents." Instead, they recast their situation, inverting it to render themselves as autonomous individuals who are able to harvest whatever they need from "obliging markets," "state banks," and others. Living in the present, they have a specific set of orientations to "time, person, and community," and explicitly contrast their life lived "in the short term" to the "longer term orientation of their neighbours": those who represent " 'respectable' ways of life" (Day et al. 1999, 2). Furthermore, for these people, "institutions associated with the long term come to be tainted by their associations with the state, with more powerful neighbours, and with processes of social control."

This account may, in retrospect, seem overly concerned with pinning specific characteristics onto particularly defined categories of people. Its emphasis on makeshift forms of reckoning resonates, however, with the attitudes and practices of some of the marginal or vulnerable people described in this book. But might it be that the very process of receiving and relying on advice draws these short-term-oriented welfare beneficiaries closer to the bureaucratic worldview? In broad contrast to the approach embodied by the two self-help examples mentioned above—and others drawn from the book—is the perspective taken by those who attempt to aid and facilitate the activities, while also defending the rights and income streams, of their clients from lower down the socioeconomic ladder. Those they advise, or whom they represent in court or through policy fora, may become reliant on institutional support for advice, counsel, and the like and are drawn into the ambit of these state-oriented and bureaucratic realities. Those who, in contrast, are not well placed to connect to these frameworks have an ambivalence, however. They *do* depend on state-provisioned types of welfare payments, but they are also left outside the most paternalistic and protective aspects of these and must "fend for themselves" when push comes to shove.

Advisers and Intermediaries

People who provide advice and support are an important topic of the book. In South Africa they include community paralegals, NGO officers, and employees of private financial companies, where in the UK the role of trained advisers working for Citizens Advice or debt advice organizations is most prominent. They also, in both settings, may include human rights lawyers and others whose concern or professional duties regarding the rights of less well-off citizens place their activities within institutionalized settings like the law courts, government departments, and ombuds offices. All of these may be regarded as intermediaries, working either voluntarily or as professionals, whose expertise is informed—and tempered—by the empathy they develop for their clients (James & Killick 2012).

My emphasis on the various forms of clawing back is one that brings together people from these disparate backgrounds: one set attempting to negotiate livelihoods largely unaided, the other acting where possible to help that
negotiation. Between these two apparently different perspectives lie a range of
intermediary positions, often facilitated by the interactions between the two
polarities.

Seen from one perspective, one might characterize these interactions as
themselves embodying acts of comparison, as I observed in a recent chapter (James 2022b). To oversimplify somewhat: because advisors, paralegals
and lawyers start from generalities and the recipients of their counsel often
start from individualized practices, comparison pushes them in different di-
rections. In the everyday life of such encounters, there are forces that propel
people (often the former) towards abstraction and generalization in their com-
parisons, while countervailing forces propel others (often the latter) towards
particularism or piecemeal pragmatism, even inclining them against—or
blinding them to—all generalizing forms of comparison.

Comparison, as embodied in the actions of the various agents discussed
in these chapters, connects to the version of perspectivism suggested to me
by Geertz's insights on the *sūq*. There are people in marginal spaces (Day et
al. 1999)—below the radar, relatively speaking—who may be unable or even
unwilling to seek help, like some of the South African interlocutors in Chapters
1 and 2. They appear to be the ones for whom comparative (read rationally
oriented, financially literate) viewpoints hold little real value. The book has
shown how many of these have needed to develop their own approach in which
both economic and social elements (including clashing and incommensurate
time scales) converge, rather than achieving some homogenizing overarching
vision of the most sensible way to behave. Conversely, those for whom
documentation, and hence proof, exist (such as those who provided a paper
trail of evidence for the court case of Chapter 3, and those whose official letters
were required in order to push back against undue demands in Chapters 4
and 5) can derive some benefit from getting a broader insight into their
dilemmas. Although we may think of "advice encounters," with their case-
by-case approach, as piecemeal and unlikely to yield broader perspectives, it is
when institutions—like the policy units of the UK's Citizens Advice, or South
Africa's judicial system—come into play, that such local-level issues may be
ramped up to the level of broader justice and government policy.

Moderating this perhaps overly binary depiction, it is often in redistributive encounters themselves that discrepant points of view—opposed

perspectives—can come together, or even switch sides. Moreover, the two kinds of scenarios—self-help autonomy and expertly aided protection—may have more in common than first appears to be the case. In both, albeit in different ways, there is a toggling between predictable and rational outcomes and those in which unknown and unanticipated eventualities unsettle these. For a grant recipient or borrower in South Africa, the loans and repayments ordered via EFTs tend to be regular and known, although they are managed by high-tech systems beyond the borrower's control. The informal loans from moneylenders will rack up unreasonable and unregulated amounts of interest, but are somewhat more under a debtor's own management in that she can operationalize them when necessary, often borrowing from a known person or savings club in the community (Chapters 1 and 2). In the UK, by contrast, benefits payments are intended and expected to be regular, predictable, and calculated through bureaucratic formulae. What makes them less so is the uncertainties introduced by the shifting membership of households, or because welfare payments must be juggled against the wages earned, often through zero-hours contracts that constantly change (Chapters 1 and 5). Here it is the state welfare system that, firstly, creates debt and, secondly, causes confusion and unpredictability because of unexpected timing. In some cases, clients may even become enabled to take a generalized, comparative view while those helping them become less so as their sensibilities are "blunted by the exigencies of the audit culture they are forced to operationalize." Realizing that "few if any structural changes are likely, these advisers can find themselves operating more 'by rote' than recognizing the bigger picture" (James 2022b, 113–114).

Calculative Logics and Techno-Politics

The answers to questions posed by the autonomy/protection dichotomy need also to be inflected by an account of what happens when householders are confronted by high-tech automation. Seen from one perspective, such automation undermines the kinds of group action that might be aimed at expressing or achieving popular sovereignty. Von Schnitzler uses the term "techno-politics" to describe how issues once at the level of grassroots mobilization are reframed as the terrain of "a diverse array of experts, including engineers, utility officials or local bureaucrats."[1] When governments or companies use high-tech solutions, aimed at "financial inclusion," this enables them to perform manipulations in the tech space that threaten to take away the options, not only for group action but also for individual maneuver of a non-formal kind, by those recently included. So, for example, transferring many grant recipients to the EPE Green Card, as happened in South Africa (Chapter 2), gave them the prospect of an important element of such inclusion—but also made it difficult to withdraw or retreat once it had been achieved. I came across numerous individuals who, offered almost instantaneous access to such facilities, later found it virtually impossible to cancel their accounts—effectively, to "re-exclude" themselves. In the UK, having benefits paid electronically meant an easy flow of money into beneficiaries' accounts. Those in charge of the tech space, however, were able to initiate deductions, diverting repayments from one income stream to another, when it was claimed that beneficiaries had been "overpaid." Equally, having a prepayment meter installed for electricity allegedly enabled people to budget and *avoid* having debts accrue by month's end. But here, too, the funds were able to be diverted by creditors to pay off existing arrears (Chapter 5).

These actions undertaken by tech experts might seem to be motivated by malign intentions. But what about those who do well-meaning things for others poorer than they, who might also embrace some aspects of auto-mated calculation? Relying on the objectivity of numbers and percentages, they apportion, and calculate as percentages, the monies that those people have (whether wages, grants, or debts). In the case of grants, assumptions are made—often in a rhetorical way—about how much is required to cope with the basics of life. South Africa's Department of Social Security ruled, in pro-tectionist spirit, that no more than 10 percent may be deducted from a person's grant (Chapter 2). In the case of wages, regulations were passed following the emoluments attachment order court case, stipulating that no more than 25 percent of a person's wage may be repaid using such orders (Chapter 3). But those who have studied low-wage, low-income households show how these householders devise their own strategies around such things (de L'Estoile 2024; Wilkis 2017). In such cases, people's valuing of autonomy and control, and their dependence on future providence, can vie with paternalistic or pro-tectionist impulses (with their rigid calculations) over the minimum needed for a sustainable livelihood in the here and now.

There is a related point, also concerned with time and temporality. It con-nects to whether or not money is seen as flattening out all social relations and turning them into a single "objective" measure. When lawyers or judges choose to represent the sum of money that a person owes, or is paid by their employer, by reference to what they might have bought had it not been looted or diverted, they are denying the fungibility of money by transforming it, rhetorically, into the things it should have been able to buy, as seen in Chapter 3. When financial companies (Chapters 2 and 3) or governments (Chapter 5) grab a salary or grant or welfare benefit by diverting it into a deduction that is reframed as a "repayment," it is being metaphorically and morally recalibrated as "what is due to us" rather than "what you have a right to." Here, what is of crucial importance is time as a vector whose passing can materially affect whether there is money or not. Likewise, in the case of Mpho in Chapter 2, different timeframes determine an intricate and seasonally influenced pattern of debts and repayments.

Paperwork, statements of account, and the like might lend themselves to an interpretation that stresses machinic aspects, automation, and the power of technologies untrammeled by human intervention. But it is in the hands of human agents—those set on making deductions or those opposed to them—that these documents and high-tech interventions find their real significance: either as collateral enabling a loan, or as repositories of dignity (Marks, forthcoming) and the right to claw back what is due.

Reclaiming the Commons—or Not?

Let us return to the topic of redistribution. An important question is whether the public good and a reclaiming of the commons must of necessity be enabled by joint and solidary action—for example, by those at the "bottom of the pile"—or whether the seemingly more individualized "redistributive encounters" I have documented here can be considered to be important in their own right. Ferguson, towards the end of *Give a Man a Fish*, advocates expanding cash transfers so as to take them "beyond the merely ameliorative and largely apolitical aims that govern current schemes" so that they "become instead sites for the development of a potent new distributive politics" (2015, 188). He quotes political analyst Steven Friedman, who says that those requiring that recipients work for their grants (in order to show they deserve them) are practicing a kind of Victorian morality. This position, says Friedman, fails to recognize that the poor can make their own decisions about what to do and how to act: something akin to the self-help approach I have demonstrated in Chapters 1 and 2. Giving out cash transfers, Friedman maintains, is the only system that recognizes this. Such a stance is perhaps commensurate with the "autonomy" side of the dichotomy outlined earlier, and with the position taken by South Africa's Department of Trade, Industry, and Competition, which viewed the right to trade and make independent financial decisions as an inalienable one guaranteed by the country's new constitution (Chapter 2).

However, the other side of that dichotomy—that is the need for "expertly aided protection," which aligns with South Africa's Department of Social Development and with the UK's original vision of a welfare state that advisers are still struggling to retain—comes into play when one recalls a point also made in Chapter 2. I mentioned there that Ferguson, in predicting how South Africa's social grants system might furnish opportunities for collective action and form the basis for citizenship, had not been well placed to anticipate subsequent developments. He could not have been expected to predict how these same grants would end up serving as loan security used by large financial companies to tempt recipients into borrowing (and to guarantee repayment). A critical account of this process, drawing on research by Torkelson (2020), claims that it opened up "a new market for formal creditors to tap into" by transforming "social entitlements into collateral for credit" (Nilsen 2020, 14). The distribution of these grants, claims Alf Nilsen, has done nothing to help "restructure" or "push back the frontiers of capitalist power" (Esping-Andersen, cited in Nilsen 2020, 16). The implication is that only collaborative or joint action can achieve such a pushback. A focus on the potential promised by grants, in contrast, is unlikely to form the basis for a truly "oppositional political project." Ferguson's thoughts on this were, however, more nuanced than Nilsen allows. Ferguson acknowledges, for example, that such grants—according to authors such as David Neves and co-authors (2009)—may merely offer a sustainable poverty rather than the transformative possibility of a non-capitalist future (Ferguson 2015, 207). But he nonetheless suggests that obtaining a fair share can have an empowering effect. In another publication, Ferguson explicitly reminds us that the livelihoods and modes of distribution he is discussing have "little to do with wage labor" (2019, 18), and hence that politics here are not those driven by classic forms of political action, such as the withholding of such labor from capitalist employers. He also asserts that "non-capitalist elements," here, are already "in ascendance, not decline" (2019, 17).

Let us explore further the claims about an "oppositional political project": what might this look like? In the US, a 1970s debt activist movement launched communal protests against racial discrimination by banks and lending institutions. By striving to invert the classic inequality between lender and borrower through their community reinvestment movement, they established new grounds for "economic citizenship" (Krippner 2017, 35). In the UK, several organizations—Jubilee Debt Campaign, Debt Resistance UK, Debt Justice, the New Economics Foundation, and others—have, albeit in a different way, voiced similar claims, calling for household debt to be written off. But one drawback of such movements, however powerful their demands, is that they tend to motivate on the grounds of debt alone, without recognizing its interplay with the other two livelihood sources explored in this book: work and welfare. Encompassing problems of debt *alongside* welfare were assertions made by members of the "Hands Off Our Grants" campaign (see Figure 2.2 in Chapter 2), prompted in South Africa by the streamlined transfer of *welfare* payments into the hands of financial companies as *debt* repayments. As with the US debt activists, this campaign was likewise motivated by a sense that what grant recipients rightfully owned—"our" grants, perhaps "our" fair share—was being unjustly alienated (see Chapter 2).

Let us then revisit the question of how and whether an oppositional political project—one that encompasses all three in my triad of livelihood sources—might arise. There are hints of such a project. The onset of social grants in South Africa, and their transformation into loan security, has meant that whatever robust efforts are made are those devoted to securing or clawing back what is rightfully theirs. Likewise, the erosion of welfare payments once regarded as part of a publicly provided resource in the UK has required a significant struggle to retain access to these. In the face of automated deductions by financial companies (in the former case) and the state (in the latter), the "new commons" can only be secured, and access to them maintained, by continued and persistent intervention. It requires ongoing distributional work rather than being achieved in a once-off achievement of shifted class power. In other words, accessing the "share" is not enough: there is a constant struggle to defend that share. And that struggle perhaps needs to be seen as an oppositional project in and of itself.

Is it then the case that what remains as a space for political action in contemporary situations consists merely of networks of individuals pursuing "self-help," or of the intermediaries in government, market, and civil society who take up these causes on behalf of others? An insightful suggestion by von Schnitzler seems to provide an answer:

> [M]odernist political idioms of popular sovereignty, social citizenship, and collective freedom have lost some of their previous resonance and numerous

questions have arisen about the ability of the formal political sphere to effectively represent citizens' multiple desires and demands.

Scholars and practitioners should, she suggests, attend to "less visible, seemingly apolitical spheres as locations where popular politics unfolds and citizenship is expressed, negotiated and claimed."[2] The actions of clawing back outlined in this book, I maintain, amount to one such sphere.

Notes

Introduction

1. This is captured, for example, in the introduction to a recent special issue of *Global Social Policy:* "Reconfiguring Labour and Welfare in the Global South."

2. The subsequent migration of the inhabitants of some of these countries to metropolitan heartlands must be partly understood against this backdrop. It is also important to note that the effects of post-1980s structural adjustment programs further intensified the pull of people, as migrant workers, from the Global South to sites of commerce in the Global North. Shortly thereafter, ironically, austerity programs, modeled on structural adjustment, began to be rolled out in these metropolitan settings as well (Powers & Rakopoulos 2019).

3. Some maintain that welfare provision, in the course of these migrations and transformations, has simultaneously morphed into something that barely resembles its earlier iteration(s). But it should be borne in mind how short-lived and geographically restricted those original forms of provision actually were. In being shipped to other shores, such models have—despite or perhaps even because of responsiveness to populist demand, and their strategic use as a means to enhance political legitimacy, perhaps as in Bismarck's original design—ended up excluding many, especially internal or transnational migrants, from gaining access.

4. Here, the move from Bismarckian to Beveridgian models seems complete (Georges 2024).

5. Thinking of the relation between "waged" and "wageless" life in a single frame is a reformulation of what Marxist social scientists earlier called the "articulation of modes of production." Many analysts have spoken of activities such as small-scale family farming, apparently conducted outside of recognizably capitalist frameworks, as in fact subordinate to those frameworks. Such kinship-based or informal activities, seen from this perspective, serve to subsidize capitalists' profits by allowing them to

pay wages lower than those required for the reproduction of the labor force (Wolpe 1972). Similar arguments were advanced by feminist anthropologists who argued that labor—framed as taking place within the boundaries of home-based groups and separate from the wider world of paid work, government, or public affairs—was in fact essential to the functioning of that world. Non-commodified activities—often seen as precapitalist—were subsumed by commodified, capitalist formations; household labor was seen by such analysts as intrinsic to capitalism and exploited by it (see Zaloom & James 2023 for a fuller discussion). Once that reproduction started to be provided through more formal redistributive mechanisms, such as state-provided welfare payments or welfare provision, one might argue, it became social policy.

6. The proceedings appeared in Hann & James 2024.

7. Both countries, at the time of writing in 2024, had just experienced electoral change, but it was too early to track the effects. The dwindling of the ANC majority in South Africa resulted in a coalition with the opposition Democratic Alliance, while in the UK the Conservative government was shown the door when the Labour Party won a historic number of seats in Parliament.

8. Zero-hours contracts are also known as casual contracts; they are usually for "piece work" or "on call" work. This means "they are on call to work when you need them, you do not have to give them work, they do not have to do work when asked." https://www.gov.uk/contract-types-and-employer-responsibilities/zero-hour-con tracts (accessed September 29, 2024).

Chapter 1

1. Pharie Sefali, Money Lender Targets Social Grant Beneficiaries, *GroundUp*, July 21, 2015. https://www.groundup.org.za/article/money-lender-targets-socialgrant-benefi ciaries_3140/ (accessed January 14, 2020); see also James, Neves, & Torkelson 2020, 30.

2. Debt advice session with Shajida Ali, London, January 17, 2017.

3. Much of the material in this section is drawn from James, Neves, & Torkelson n.d.

4. Citizens Advice, On the Edge: Insecure Work in the Pandemic. https://www.cit izensadvice.org.uk/Global/CitizensAdvice/Work%20Publications/On%20the%20 Edge_%20Insecure%20work%20in%20the%20pandemic.pdf (accessed November 11th, 2024).

5. https://www.ethnicity-facts-figures.service.gov.uk/style-guide/writing-about-eth nicity/ (accessed September 26, 2024). This usage has since been discontinued.

6. In England and Wales, lower-tier local authorities are borough, county, or district councils. They are funded through a blend of central government grants, the council tax they levy, parking charges, and business rates. Their responsibilities include (but are not limited to) administering housing and council tax benefits, administering social housing, and providing emergency shelter.

7. The Zulu word *mashonisa* may be translated as "one who impoverishes" or who "takes and continues to take indefinitely" (Krige 2011, 144). In popular parlance the plural is *mashonisas* (Krige 2011, 151; Siyongwana 2004, 851).

8. James, Neves, & Torkelson 2020; Nilsen 2020; Torkelson 2020, 2021; Vally 2016.

9. James, Neves, & Torkelson n.d., 20–22 (Botshabelo), 29 (Delft), 70 (Hammansk-raal), 107 (Khayelitsha), 178 (Uitenhage).

10. The insistence on pay slips is of course intended as proof that the borrower will be in a position to repay. It is also, however, evidence of the society's productivist bias (Ferguson 2015).

11. James, Neves, & Torkelson n.d., 20–22, 107 (Khayelitsha).

12. The word "legacy" is important here. According to Menahem, "social tradition persists in the old-established social State of the United Kingdom"; he speaks of "the importance of social incomes inherited from the Beveridge Plan" as a kind of inheritance (2007, 97).

13. Patrick Butler, Carers Threatened with Prosecution over Minor Breaches of UK Benefit Rules, *The Guardian,* April 7, 2024. https://www.theguardian.com/society/2024/apr/07/unpaid-carers-allowance-payment-prosecution-earnings-rules?CMP=Share_iOSApp_Other (accessed July 22, 2024).

14. Yusuf, North London Muslim Community Centre, November 5, 2015. The case is discussed in its wider context in Forbess & James 2017, 19.

Chapter 2

1. Leila Patel & Yolanda Sadie, Over 26 Million South Africans Get a Social Grant. Fear of Losing the Payment Used to Be a Reason for Voting ANC, but No Longer, Study, *The Conversation,* May 14, 2024. https://theconversation.com/over-26-million-south-africans-get-a-social-grant-fear-of-losing-the-payment-used-to-be-a-reason-to-vote-for-the-anc-but-no-longer-study-229771#:~:text=The%20country's%20social%20grants%20system,with%20disabilities%20and%20the%20unemployed (accessed September 27, 2024).

2. The book has also been seen as a work of Cold War scholarship that sought to make Weber's insights useful, in which features of local culture had to be known before they could be reformed and changed. Hans Steinmuller, personal communication, November 7, 2023.

3. Friedrich Hayek, often mistakenly taken as exemplifying neoliberal market ideology, made similar observations. The market, he showed, is not necessarily a space in which all information is available to everyone: instead it can involve partial, often local, information, to which only some are party. Jonathan Rée & Thomas Jones, The Hayek Puzzle, *London Review of Books* podcast. https://www.lrb.co.uk/podcasts-and-videos/podcasts/the-lrb-podcast/the-hayek-puzzle (accessed July 18, 2024).

4. For more on the complexities of this case and the legal challenges mounted by Black Sash, see Black Sash 2022.

5. In similar vein, in a co-written paper with Sam Kirwan on debt advice encounters in the UK being sought by welfare-dependent people with precarious jobs, we showed how "welfare" is never simply or straightforwardly delivered by a single authority to a unitary recipient and in a neatly distinct payment. Instead, it is mediated by advisers using a complex set of spreadsheets and calculations, and involving the central state, local authorities, and market actors. Again, some of these involve yield-

ing necessary information while others involve withholding it (James & Kirwan 2019).

6. Those running the training workshops have subsequently produced a report (James et al. 2024).

7. During one of the early training workshops for paralegals, the *mashonisas* raised more queries than the advisers. This suggested that such training, by giving information about regularizing and registering their lending practices, might perhaps aid borrowers indirectly. Subsequent work with Black Sash has revealed more about the complexities of informal moneylending (James et al. 2024); the report notes the important role advisers can play in liaising between borrowers and those lenders who charge the highest rates of interest.

Chapter 3

1. Von Schnitzler (2016, 59) traces the origins of such paternalism, and its supposed evolution through which black residents would be gradually exposed to "free market forces," in the ideas of Afrikaner economist and government adviser Jan Lombard.

2. The material analyzed is drawn from court judgments, the case files held by Stellenbosch University Law Clinic (SULC), formerly—and at the time of the case—known as University of Stellenbosch Law Clinic (USLAC), and the PhD thesis by one of its officers, Stephan van der Merwe, as well as from interviews with some of those involved in the case.

3. *University of Stellenbosch Legal Aid Clinic and Others v Minister of Justice and Correctional Services and Others.* http://www.saflii.org/za/cases/ZAWCHC/2015/99 .html (accessed July 17, 2024). In 2015, this equated to about £82 million or $126 million.

4. Magistrates' Courts Act 32 of 1944. https://www.gov.za/documents/magistrates% E2%80%99-courts-act-19-may-1944-0000 (accessed July 17, 2024).

5. *University of Stellenbosch Legal Aid Clinic and Others v Minister of Justice and Correctional Services and Others; Association of Debt Recovery Agents NPC v University of Stellenbosch Legal Aid Clinic and Others; Mavava Trading 279 (Pty) Ltd and Others v University of Stellenbosch Legal Aid Clinic and Others.* http://www.saflii.org/ za/cases/ZACC/2016/32.html (accessed July 17, 2024).

6. Courts of Law Amendment Act 7 of 2017. https://www.gov.za/documents/courts -law-amendment-act-7-2017-english-afrikaans-2-aug-2017-0000 (accessed July 17, 2024).

7. The table was compiled from the SULC documents, but these did not furnish a complete set of figures. In 2015, R10 was equal to £0.51 or $0.79. An applicant in a legal case is the one who starts proceedings; he or she may do so on behalf of others. A respondent is the one against whom the case is being brought.

8. Barbara Maregele, Debt Collecting Firm Flemix Fined for Dodgy Practice, *Daily Maverick*, February 6, 2020. https://www.dailymaverick.co.za/article/2020-02-06-debt -collecting-firm-flemix-fined-for-dodgy-practice/ (accessed July 17, 2024). The diagram in this article shows how Malcolm Rees attempted to make sense of the connections between some of these debt collection agencies and the law firm that was acting on their behalf.

9. Affidavit by XV, SULC documents, 335–341.

10. Affidavit by Kruger van der Walt, SULC documents, 19, 69.

11. Affidavit by Aletta Flemix-Jordaan, SULC documents, 701–716, quote at 716.

12. Affidavit by Marius Jonkers, SULC documents, 919.

13. Julia Kagan, Debt Buyer: Who They Are and How They Work, *Investopedia*, March 19, 2024. https://www.investopedia.com/terms/d/debt-buyer.asp#:~:text=Why%20Debt%20Buyers%20Are%20Used,recoup%20some%20of%20the%20loss (accessed July 17, 2024): "If a lender . . . is unable to collect payment on outstanding debt according to the terms of their financing, they may seek to recoup some of the loss. There are instances in which a lender sees limited or no opportunity to recover the funds within the time frame originally outlined when the loan or credit was taken out. Rather than continue to wait for the debtor to pay off the delinquent debt in full, the lender could turn to a debt buyer and transfer ownership of that account for a smaller return."

14. Odette Geldenhuys, Cape Town, November 21, 2017.

15. https://groundup.org.za/article/debt-collecting-firm-guilty-dodgy-practice-finds-legal-practice-council/#:~:text=Flemix%20%26%20Associates%2C%20a%20firm%20of,far%20from%20where%20they%20live. (accessed November 11th, 2024).

16. Affidavits by applicants, SULC documents, 376–700.

17. Sune van der Merwe, December 27, 2017. This and other quotes are from the same interview.

18. SULC documents, 1184, 1194, 1204, 1209.

19. Affidavit by Karin Ellerd, SULC documents, 1533.

20. Odette Geldenhuys, Cape Town, November 2, 2017. A charge of "reckless lending" must be proved using documentation issued by the original lender.

21. Geoff Budlender, Cape Town, December 12, 2017.

22. Quotes are from affidavits by Marius Jonker and Aletta Flemix, SULC documents, 908, 1056–1057. For similar points in a case in the US, see Stephan van der Merwe (2021, 12 fn166).

23. According to SULC's Stephan van der Merwe, it resulted from "the development of common-law procedural affordances supporting a predominantly civil-law substantive system" (2021).

24. Geoff Budlender, Cape Town, December 12, 2017.

25. *Coetzee v Government of the Republic of South Africa; Matiso and Others v Commanding Officer Port Elizabeth Prison and Others.* http://www.saflii.org/za/cases/ZACC/1995/7.html (accessed July 17, 2024).

26. Clark Gardner, Cape Town, November 21, 2017.

27. Sune van der Merwe, Stellenbosch, December 13, 2017.

28. *Lonmin Ltd v CG Steyn Inc t/a Steyn Attorneys and Others.* https://www.saflii.org/za/cases/ZANWHC/2018/10.html (accessed July 17, 2024).

29. The case was dismissed on the grounds that a variety of parties "that have a direct and substantial interest and/or parties that have a vital interest in the litigation and possible result" had not been invited to join it (Stephan van der Merwe 2021, 116; see 108–120 for a detailed discussion of the legal dimensions and ramifications of the case).

30. *University of Stellenbosch Law Clinic v National Credit Regulator.* http://www.saflii.org/za/cases/ZAWCHC/2019/172.html (accessed July 17, 2024).

31. *Bayport Securitisation Limited v University of Stellenbosch Law Clinic.* http://www.saflii.org/za/cases/ZASCA/2021/156.html (accessed July 17, 2024).

32. This and subsequent quotes are from Sune van der Merwe, Stellenbosch, December 13, 2017.

33. Clark Gardner, Cape Town, November 21, 2017.

34. The view that workers "own" the product of their labor, Krippner points out, has long motivated labor mobilization. In capitalist relations, the payment of a wage compensates for the fact that the worker does not own the product of her labor. "In contrast, the creditor's reliance on collateral means that both parties to the transaction accept the borrower's status as (partial) owner" (2017, 12).

35. Clark Gardner, Cape Town, November 21, 2017.

36. Buyeleni Sibanyoni, Dewald van Rensburg, & Magnificent Mndebele, Past Sins Come Back to Haunt Microlenders, with Capitec on the Frontline, *Daily Maverick,* July 5, 2024. https://amabhungane.org/past-sins-come-back-to-haunt-microlenders -with-capitec-on-the-frontline/ (accessed July 24, 2024).

Chapter 4

1. Yusuf, North London Muslim Community Center, November 5, 2015.

2. Some of the material in this section is drawn from an article by Alice Forbess and me (Forbess & James 2017) and our unpublished paper (Forbess & James n.d.).

3. Andy Benson, National Coalition for Independent Action, London, December 3, 2014.

4. Funded legal advice, establishing citizen equality before the law and enabling fair access to services, was provided by the welfare state, as laid out in the 1949 Legal Aid and Advice Act (Biggs 2011; Forbess & James 2014). In the 1970s its scope was widened to include social welfare law. UK Law Centres were established, staffed with specialists in the areas of the law relevant to poor people's lives. Sources of advice diversified while their funding was restricted under the Thatcher and Major Conservative governments, whose efforts to slim the state suggested a new role for the voluntary sector, initiating a trend towards government by NGO (Gladstone 1999, 88). The legal aid system was formalized and brought under central government control in 1988, placing the Legal Aid Board (LAB) in charge of commissioning and early forms of franchising and quality control, ending the Law Society's administration of the scheme (Moorhead 2001, 548–549).

5. NPM was introduced in the name of (1) fiscal restraint, (2) the alleged necessity of reducing state service provision, (3) the idea of accountability to taxpayers and in opposition to "cosy cultures of professional self-regulation." The idea was that money must be seen to be spent "economically, efficiently and effectively" (Power 1999, 44). After its introduction in the UK, it spread worldwide (Pollitt et al. 1999).

6. It abolished the Legal Aid Board in 1999 and replaced it with the LSC (Legal Services Commission), which was given charge of legal aid budgets, commissioning, quality marks, and the assessment of bills.

7. Jen Stewart, London, May 29, 2014.

8. This and other quotes are from an interview with Andy Benson, December 3, 2014.

9. Simi Ryatt and Celia Cleave, Hammersmith and Fulham CA, August 11, 2014. CA

(Citizens Advice, formerly Citizens Advice Bureau) is a prominent UK advice charity with a national office and a network of local ones. See https://www.citizensadvice.org .uk/about-us/ (accessed July 7, 2024).

10. Some of the information in this section is drawn from that paper commissioned by Black Sash (James et al. 2021).

11. The Financial Services and Markets Act, 2000: https://www.legislation.gov.uk /ukpga/2000/8/schedule/1A; The Financial Services Act of 2010: https://www.legisla tion.gov.uk/ukpga/2010/28/schedule/1. Other documents can be found on the website of the Financial Conduct Authority: https://www.fca.org.uk; and the Money and Pensions Service: https://maps.org.uk/en/our-work/our-debt-work (accessed September 29, 2024).

12. For example, in 2010–11, it was calculated that the 470 small "payment institutions" would have contributed £4,700 towards recovery of the costs of debt advice (FSA 2010, 31).

13. https://moneyandpensionsservice.org.uk/who-we-are/ (accessed November 3, 2023).

14. On the levy for 2020, see https://www.fca.org.uk/publication/consultation/cp 20-06.pdf; and https://www.fca.org.uk/publication/policy/ps20-07.pdf (accessed November 3, 2023).

15. Written communication with Michael Agboh Davison, October 11, 2020. See research published by the IMA (Institute of Money Advisers) that underlines this: https://www.i-m-a.org.uk/workload-conditions-and-wellbeing-in-the-money-advice -sector/ (accessed July 18, 2024).

16. Ryan Davey, personal communication.

17. Written communication with Michael Agboh Davison, October 11, 2020.

18. https://www.foryoubyyou.org.uk/about-us/who-we-help (accessed July 18, 2024).

19. https://perennial.org.uk/ (accessed July 18, 2024).

20. Maurice Wren, Refugee Council, London, May 27, 2014.

21. THHAL Advisory Group Meeting, Brady Arts Center, March 3, 2015.

22. As noted in Chapters 1 and 5, this tax, given the devolution of a benefit designed to aid those who struggle to pay it, has become one of the primary debts faced by CA clients (Lane et al. 2018).

23. Minutes, Welfare Reform Operational Group, Kingston, March 3, 2015; Complex Cases Protocol, Welfare Reform Operational Group, Kingston, February 2, 2014.

Chapter 5

1. This is a move away from the original Beveridgian model of the welfare state: of "a lifetime of shared risks—a world in which you could not neatly divide the population into those who paid and those who received" (Hills 2015, 4; see also Fraser & Gordon 1994, 323).

2. Adviser, Hammersmith and Fulham CA, August 28, 2014.

3. We might note the unreliability of (semi) official public-private partnership systems for verifying beneficiaries' circumstances. As a possible means to stabilize or "sort out" her income (James & Kirwan 2019), Donna was waiting to hear whether

she qualified for a DLA (now replaced by PIP). The agency to which the government had outsourced the task of assessing eligibility for this and other benefits, ATOS, was discredited and its contract was removed. John Pring, "ATOS Is Left with Blood on Its Hands" After DWP Calls Time on Its 20 Years of Assessments, *Disability News Service*, October 19, 2023. https://www.disabilitynewsservice.com/atos-is-left-with-blood-on-its-hands-after-dwp-calls-time-on-its-20-years-of-assessments/ (accessed November 6, 2024).

4. If a family is relying on commercially provided credit, for example, an adviser is not permitted to fill in a common financial statement that includes non-contributing non-dependents, as it would not be accepted by creditors.

5. Patrick Butler, Carers Threatened with Prosecution over Minor Breaches of UK Benefit Rules, *The Guardian*, April 7, 2024. https://www.theguardian.com/society/2024/apr/07/unpaid-carers-allowance-payment-prosecution-earnings-rules?CMP=Share_iOSApp_Other (accessed July 22, 2024).

6. Ed Davey, Leader of the Liberal Democrats, Prime Minister's Questions. https://www.facebook.com/EdwardjDavey/videos/490506183627632/ (accessed November 11th, 2024).

7. This is a means through which a person who disagrees with a decision about benefits, tax credits, or child maintenance "can ask for the decision to be looked at again." https://www.gov.uk/mandatory-reconsideration (accessed June 20, 2023).

8. Antina von Schnitzler, Democracy's Infrastructure. Democracy in Africa, n.d. http://democracyinafrica.org/democracys-infrastructure/ (accessed June 16, 2023).

9. Julia Kollewe, UK Energy Suppliers to End Prepayment Meter Installation in Vulnerable Homes, *The Guardian*, February 10, 2023. https://www.theguardian.com/business/2023/feb/10/uk-energy-suppliers-to-end-prepayment-meter-installation-in-vulnerable-homes (accessed June 16, 2023); Anne Pardoe, It's Time to Stop Forcing People onto Prepayment Meters—Here's Why, *We Are Citizens Advice*, January 12, 2023. https://wearecitizensadvice.org.uk/its-time-to-stop-forcing-people-onto-prepayment-meters-here-s-why-69bf0ea21db5 (accessed June 19, 2023).

10. Alex Lawson, UK Energy Suppliers Stop Clawing Back Debts via Prepayment Meters, *The Guardian*, January 15, 2023. https://www.theguardian.com/business/2023/jan/15/uk-energy-suppliers-stop-clawing-back-debt-prepayment-meters (accessed September 28, 2024).

11. Tony Carnie, Top SA Scientists Present Action Plan to Fight Nationwide Cholera Outbreak, *Daily Maverick*, June 7, 2023. https://www.dailymaverick.co.za/article/2023-06-07-top-sa-scientists-present-action-plan-to-fight-nationwide-cholera-outbreak/ (accessed June 13, 2023).

Conclusion

1. Antina von Schnitzler, Democracy's Infrastructure. *Democracy in Africa*, n.d. http://democracyinafrica.org/democracys-infrastructure/ (accessed June 16, 2023).

2. Antina von Schnitzler, Democracy's Infrastructure. *Democracy in Africa*, n.d. http://democracyinafrica.org/democracys-infrastructure/ (accessed June 16, 2023).

References

Adkins, Lisa. 2017. Speculative Futures in the Time of Debt. *Sociological Review* 65: 448–462.

Alexander, Catherine. 2010. Third Sector. In *The Human Economy: A Citizens' Guide*, eds. Keith Hart, Jean-Louis Laville, & Antonio David Cattani, 213–224. Cambridge, UK: Polity Press.

Ardener, Shirley. 1964. The Comparative Study of Rotating Credit Associations. *Journal of the Royal Anthropological Institute* 94(2): 201–229.

———. 2010. Microcredit, Money Transfers, Women, and the Cameroon Diaspora. *Afrika Focus* 23(2): 11–24.

Ardington, Cally, David Lam, Murray Leibbrandt, & James Levinsohn. 2004. Savings, Insurance and Debt over the Post-Apartheid Period: A Review of Recent Research. *South African Journal of Economics* 72(3): 604–640.

Atfield, G., K. Brahmbhatt, & T. O'Toole. 2007. *Refugees' Experiences of Integration*. Birmingham: University of Birmingham and the Refugee Council.

Bähre, Erik. 2007. *Money and Violence: Financial Self-Help Groups in a South African Township*. Leiden: Brill.

———. 2011. Liberation and Redistribution: Social Grants, Commercial Insurance, and Religious Riches in South Africa. *Comparative Studies in Society and History* 53(2): 371–392.

———. 2020. *Ironies of Solidarity: Insurance and Financialization of Kinship in South Africa*. London: Zed Books.

Bandelj, Nina. 2020. Relational Work in the Economy. *Annual Review of Sociology* 46: 251–272.

Barchiesi, Franco. 2011. *Precarious Liberation. Workers, the State and Contested Social Citizenship in Postapartheid South Africa*. Albany: SUNY Press.

159

Bear, Laura. 2015. *Navigating Austerity: Currents of Debt Along a South Asian River.* Palo Alto: Stanford University Press.

Bear, Laura, & Nayanika Mathur. 2015. Remaking the Public Good: For a New Anthropology of Bureaucracy. *Cambridge Journal of Social Anthropology* 33(1): 18–34.

Biggs, Joanna. 2011. Who Will Get Legal Aid Now? *London Review of Books* 33(20): 19–22.

Black Sash. 2022. *Hands Off Our Grants: Defending the Constitutional Right to Social Protection in South Africa.* Cape Town: BestRed.

Bovensiepen, Judith, & Mathijs Pelkmans. 2020. Dynamics of Wilful Blindness: An Introduction. *Critique of Anthropology* 40(4): 387–402.

Breckenridge, Keith. 2014. *Biometric State: The Global Politics of Identification and Surveillance in South Africa, 1850 to the Present.* Cambridge, UK: Cambridge University Press.

———. 2019. The Global Ambitions of the Biometric Anti-Bank: Net1, Lockin and the Technologies of African Financialization. *International Review of Applied Economics* 33(1): 93–118.

Brown, Wendy. 2015. *Undoing the Demos: Neoliberalism's Stealth Revolution.* Boston: MIT Press.

Carney Ao, Terry. 2018. The New Digital Future for Welfare: Debts Without Legal Proofs or Moral Authority? *UNSW Law Journal Forum* 1: 1–16.

Carruthers, Bruce G. 2022. *The Economy of Promises: Trust, Power, and Credit in America.* Princeton: Princeton University Press.

Carter, L P R. (Lord Carter of Coles). 2006. *Legal Aid: A Market-Based Approach to Reform.* London: House of Lords. https://www.iomlawsociety.co.im/wp-content/uploads/2016/04/Appendix-13.pdf (accessed November 3, 2023).

Chang, Ha-Joon. 2022. *Edible Economics: A Hungry Economist Explains the World.* UK: Allen Lane.

Christophers, Brett, Andrew Leyshon, & Geoff Mann. 2017. Money and Finance After the Crisis: Taking Critical Stock. In *Money and Finance After the Crisis: Critical Thinking for Uncertain Times*, eds. Brett Christophers, Andrew Leyshon, & Geoff Mann, 1–40. Hoboken, NJ: Wiley Blackwell.

Clark, Christopher. 2007. *Iron Kingdom. The Rise and Downfall of Prussia, 1600–1947.* Harmondsworth: Penguin.

Clarke, John, & Janet Newman. 1997. *The Managerial State: Power, Politics and Ideology in the Remaking of Social Welfare.* London: Sage.

Cooper, Frederick. 1997. Modernising Bureaucrats, Backward Africans and the Development Concept. In *International Development and the Social Sciences: Essays on the History and Politics of Knowledge*, eds. Frederick Cooper & Randall Packard, 64–92. Berkeley: University of California Press.

———. 2002. *Africa Since 1940: The Past of the Present.* Cambridge, UK: Cambridge University Press.

Cooper, Melinda. 2014. *Cut Adrift: Families in Insecure Times.* Oakland: University of California Press.

Cunningham, Hugh. 1998. Introduction. In *Charity, Philanthropy and Reform, from the 1690s to 1850*, eds. Hugh Cunningham & Joanna Innes, 1–14. London: Macmillan.

Daniels, Reza. 2004. Financial Intermediation, Regulation and the Formal Microcredit Sector in South Africa. *Development Southern Africa* 21(5): 831–849.

Datta, Kavita. 2012. *Migrants and Their Money: Surviving Financial Exclusion*. Bristol: Policy Press.

Davey, Ryan. 2017. Polluter Pays? Understanding Austerity Through Debt Advice in the UK. *Anthropology Today* 33(5): 8–11.

———. 2022. Financialised Welfare and Its Vulnerabilities: Advice, Consumer Credit, and Church-Based Charity in the UK. *Ethnos* 87(1): 78–96.

Dawson, Hannah J. 2022. Living, Not Just Surviving: The Politics of Refusing Low-Wage Jobs in Urban South Africa. *Economy and Society* 51(3): 375–397.

Day, Sophie, Evthymios Papataxiarchis, & Michael Stewart. 1999. Consider the Lilies of the Field. In *Lilies of the Field: Marginal People Who Live for the Moment*, eds. Sophie Day, Evthymios Papataxiarchis, & Michael Stewart, 1–24. Boulder: Westview Press.

de L'Estoile, Benoît. 2024. Can Economic Anthropology Escape from Primitive Economics? Thinking Ethnographically from the Brazilian *Oikos*. In *One Hundred Years of Argonauts: Malinowski, Ethnography, and Economic Anthropology*, eds. Chris Hann & Deborah James, 161–185. New York: Berghahn Books.

Delius, Peter. 1996. *A Lion Amongst the Cattle*. Johannesburg: Ravan Press.

Denning, Michael. 2010. Wageless Life. *New Left Review* 66 (November/December): 79–96.

Donovan, Kevin. 2015. The Biometric Imaginary: Bureaucratic Technopolitics in Post-Apartheid Welfare. *Journal of Southern African Studies* 41(4): 815–833.

Elster, Jon. 1991. Local Justice: How Institutions Allocate Scarce Goods and Necessary Burdens. *European Economic Review* 35(2–3): 273–291.

Esping-Andersen, Gøsta. 1990. *The Three Worlds of Welfare Capitalism*. Princeton: Princeton University Press.

Fechter, Anne-Meike. 2020. Brokering Transnational Flows of Care: The Case of Citizen Aid. *Ethnos* 85(2): 293–308.

Ferguson, James. 2012. What Comes After the Social? Historicizing the Future of Social Assistance and Identity Registration in Africa. In *Registration and Recognition: Documenting the Person in World History*, eds. Keith Breckenridge & Simon Szreter, 495–516. London: Oxford University Press and British Academy.

———. 2015. *Give a Man a Fish: Reflections on the New Politics of Distribution*. Durham: Duke University Press.

———. 2019. Proletarian Politics Today: On the Perils and Possibilities of Historical Analogy. *Comparative Studies in Society and History* 61(1): 4–22.

Ferguson, James, & Akhil Gupta. 2002. Spatializing States: Toward an Ethnography of Neoliberal Governmentality. *American Ethnologist* 29(4): 981–1002.

Ferguson, James, & Tania Murray Li. 2018. Beyond the 'Proper Job': Political-Economic

Analysis After the Century of Labouring Man. *Working Paper 51*. Cape Town: PLAAS.

Forbess, Alice. 2022. Redistribution Dilemmas and Ethical Commitments: Advisers in Austerity Britain's Local Welfare State *Ethnos* 87(1): 42–58.

Forbess, Alice, & Deborah James. 2014. Acts of Assistance: Navigating the Interstices of the State with the Help of UK Non-Profit Legal Advisers. *Social Analysis* 58(3): 73–89.

———. n.d. Inventing Intervention in the Time of Austerity. Unpublished paper. LSE, 2016.

———. 2017. Innovation and Patchwork Partnerships: Advice Services in Austere Times. *Oñati Socio-Legal Series* [online] 7(7). http://ssrn.com/abstract=3056205 (accessed July 1, 2024).

Fouksman, Liz, & Hannah Dawson. 2024. Redistributive Politics and the Temporalities of Crisis: Covid and the Reconfiguring of Social Protection in South Africa. *Global Social Policy*. https://doi-org.gate3.library.lse.ac.uk/10.1177/14680181231201 493 (accessed July 1, 2024).

Fraser, Nancy. 2014. Can Society Be Commodities All the Way Down? Post-Polanyian Reflections on Capitalist Crisis. *Economy and Society* 43(4): 541–558.

Fraser, Nancy, & Linda Gordon. 1994. A Genealogy of Dependency: Tracing a Keyword of the U.S. Welfare State. *Signs* 19(2): 309–336.

Freund, Bill. 2010. The Social Context of African Economic Growth 1960–2008. In *The Political Economy of Africa*, ed. Vishnu Padayachee, 39–59. London: Routledge.

FSA. 2010. Consultation Paper 10/24. Regulatory Fees and Levies: Policy Proposals for 2011/12. https://webarchive.nationalarchives.gov.uk/20121119152627/http:/www.fsa.gov.uk/pubs/cp/cp10_24.pdf (accessed January 7, 2024).

Geertz, Clifford. 1962. The Rotating Credit Association: A "Middle Rung" in Development. *Economic Development and Cultural Change* 10(3): 241–263.

———. 1968. *Peddlers and Princes: Social Development and Economic Change in Two Indonesian Towns*. Chicago: University of Chicago Press.

———. 2023. *Sūq: Geertz on the Market*, ed. Lawrence Rosen. Chicago: Hau Books.

Genn, Hazel. 1999. *Paths to Justice: What People Do and Think About Going to the Law*. London: Hart.

Georges, Isabel. 2024. The Commodification of Poverty in the Global South: The Emergence of a Market of Social Policies (São Paulo, Brazil). *Global Social Policy*. https://doi.org/10.1177/14680181241263586 (accessed September 6, 2024).

Gladstone, David. 1999. *The Twentieth-Century Welfare State*. London: Macmillan.

Gregory, Chris. 2009. Whatever Happened to Householding. In *Market and Society: The Great Transformation Today*, eds. Chris Hann & Keith Hart, 133–159. Cambridge, UK: Cambridge University Press.

———. 2012. On Money Debt and Morality: Some Reflections on the Contribution of Economic Anthropology. *Social Anthropology* 20(4): 380–396.

Guérin, Isabelle. 2014. Juggling with Debt, Social Ties, and Values: The Everyday Use of Microcredit in Rural South India. *Current Anthropology* 55(Supplement 9): S40–S50.

Guérin, Isabelle, & Santosh Kumar. 2020. Unpayable Debt: Debt, Gender, and Sex in Financialized India. *American Ethnologist* 47(3): 1–15.

Guérin, Isabelle, Solène Morvant-Roux, & Magdalena Villarreal. 2013. Introduction. In *Microfinance, Debt and Over-Indebtedness: Juggling with Money,* eds. Isabelle Guérin, Solène Morvant-Roux, and Magdalena Villarreal, 1–23. London: Routledge.

Guyer, Jane. 1981. Household and Community in African Studies. *African Studies Review.* 24(2–3): 87–137.

———. 2004. *Marginal Gains: Monetary Transactions in Atlantic Africa.* Chicago: Chicago University Press

Guyer, Jane, & Pauline Peters. 1987. Introduction. *Development and Change* 18(2): 197–214.

Han, Clara. 2012. *Life in Debt: Times of Care and Violence in Neoliberal Chile.* Berkeley and Los Angeles: University of California Press.

Hann, Chris, & Keith Hart. 2009. Introduction—Learning from Polanyi. In *Market and Society: The Great Transformation Today,* eds. Chris Hann & Keith Hart. Cambridge, UK: Cambridge University Press.

———. 2011. *Economic Anthropology: History, Ethnography, Critique.* Cambridge, UK: Polity Press.

Hann, Chris, & Deborah James, eds. 2024. *One Hundred Years of Argonauts: Malinowski, Ethnography, and Economic Anthropology.* New York: Berghahn Books.

Hart, Keith. 2007. Marcel Mauss: In Pursuit of the Whole. *Comparative Studies in Society and History* 49(2): 473–485.

———. 2015. How the Informal Economy Took over the World. In *Informal Market Worlds Reader: The Architecture of Economic Pressure,* eds. Peter Moertenboeck, Helge Mooshammer, Teddy Cruz, & Fonna Forman, 33–44. Rotterdam: nai010 Publishers.

Haupt, Frans, & Hermie Coetzee. 2008. The Emoluments Attachment Order and the Employer. In *Employee Financial Wellness: A Corporate Social Responsibility,* ed. E. Crous, 81–92. Pretoria: GTZ (Deutsche Gesellschaft für Technische Zusammenarbeit).

Hills, John. 2015. *Good Times, Bad Times: The Welfare Myth of Them and Us.* Bristol: Policy Press.

Hoffman, Denise, Benjamin Fischer, John T. Jones, Andrew McGuirk, & Miriam Loewenberg. 2019. Work-Related Overpayments to Social Security Disability Insurance Beneficiaries: Prevalence and Descriptive Statistics. *Social Security Bulletin* 79(2): 65–83.

Hull, Elizabeth, & Deborah James. 2012. Introduction: Local Economies and Citizen Expectations in South Africa. *Africa* 82(1): 1–19.

IFF. 2012. User Needs from Debt Advice: Individual and Stakeholder Views. https://mascdn.azureedge.net/cms/research_feb12_iff_report.pdf (accessed November 3, 2023).

James, Deborah. 2007. *Gaining Ground? Rights and Property in South African Land Reform.* London: Routledge.

———. 2011. The Return of the Broker: Consensus, Hierarchy and Choice in South

African Land Reform *Journal of the Royal Anthropological Institute* 17(2): 318–338.

———. 2015. *Money from Nothing: Aspiration and Indebtedness in South Africa.* Stanford: Stanford University Press.

———. 2017. Deductions and Counter-Deductions in South Africa. *Hau* 7(3): 281–304.

———. 2020. Redistribution and Indebtedness: A Tale of Two Settings. In *Financialization: Relational Approaches,* eds. Chris Hann & Don Kalb, 33–44. London: Berghahn Books.

———. 2021. Life and Debt: A View from the South. *Economy and Society* 50(1): 36–56.

———. 2022a. Owing Everyone: Debt Advice in the UK's Time of Austerity. *Ethnos* 87(7): 59–77.

———. 2022b. Principles or Pragmatics? Debt Advice as a Comparative Encounter. In *How People Compare,* eds. Harry Walker & Mathijs Pelkmans, 107–127. London: Routledge.

James, Deborah, with Ryan Davey, Viviane Fernandes, Andrew Hutchison, Sam Kirwan, Lena Lavinas, & Marek Mikuš. 2021. Funding Free Debt Advice in South Africa: Lessons from the UK, Croatia and Brazil. https://www.lse.ac.uk/anthropol ogy/assets/documents/people/department-staff/Funding-debt-advice-pdf.pdf (accessed July 26, 2024).

James, Deborah, & Samuel Kirwan. 2019. "Sorting out Income": Transnational House-holding and Austerity Britain. *Social Anthropology.* doi:10.1111/1469–8676.12619

James, Deborah, & Insa Koch. 2020. Economies of Advice. In *Oxford Research Encyclopedia of Anthropology,* ed. Mark Aldenderfer. New York: Oxford University Press.

James, Deborah, David Neves, & Erin Torkelson. n.d. Consolidated Case Studies—Black Sash Reckless Lending Report. Unpublished. Cape Town: Black Sash.

———. 2020. *Social Grants: Challenging Reckless Lending in South Africa.* Cape Town: Black Sash. https://www.blacksash.org.za/images/publications/Social_Grants_-_ Challenging_Reckless_Lending_in_South_Africa_FINALCHANGES_Thurs10 092020.pdf (accessed July 26, 2024).

———. 2022. Saving, Investment, Thrift? Welfare Beneficiary Households and Borrowing in South Africa. In *Thrift and Its Paradoxes: From Domestic to Political Economy,* eds. Catherine Alexander & Daniel Sosna, 49–73. London: Berghahn Books.

James, Deborah, with Odwa Nweba, Kabelo Teme, Amanda Rinquest, & Kholiwe Dlali. 2024. *Collaborations to Curb Involuntary Indebtedness.* Cape Town: Black Sash.

James, Deborah, & Dinah Rajak. 2014. Debt or Savings? Of Migrants, Mines and Money. In *A Long Way Home: Migrant Worker Worlds, 1800–2014,* eds. Peter Delius, Laura Phillips, & Fiona Rankin-Smith, 241–253. Johannesburg: Wits University Press.

Kalb, Don. 2020. Introduction: Transitions to What? On the Social Relations of Financialization in Anthropology and History. In *Financialization: Relational Approaches,* eds. Chris Hann & Don Kalb, 1–42. New York: Berghahn Books.

Kallis, Giorgos, Susan Paulson, Giacomo D'Alisa, & Federico Demaria. 2020. *The Case for Degrowth*. London: Polity Press.

Kar, Sohini. 2013. Recovering Debts: Microfinance Loan Officers and the Work of "Proxy-Creditors" in India. *American Ethnologist* 40(3): 480–493.

———. 2018. *Financializing Poverty: Labor and Risk in Indian Microfinance*. Redwood City: Stanford University Press.

Kasmir, Sharryn, & August Carbonella, eds. 2014. *Blood and Fire: Towards a Global Anthropology of Labour*. New York: Berghahn Books.

Killick, Evan. 2014. Whose Truth Is It Anyway? *Anthropology of This Century* 9. http://aotcpress.com/articles/truth/ (accessed July 26, 2024).

Kirwan, Samuel. 2018. On "Those Who Shout the Loudest": The Work of Disrupting Attachments. *Geoforum* 19: 318–326. https://doi.org/10.1016/j.geoforum.2018.05.005

———. 2021a. Between a Knock at the Door and a Knock to Your Score: Re-Thinking "Governing Through Debt" Through the Hopeful "Imaginaries" of UK Debtors. *Journal of Cultural Economy* 14(2): 159–175.

———. 2021b. Benefits Overpayments and the Criminalisation of Female Poverty. In *Oppressed by Debt: Government and the Justice System as a Creditor of the Poor*, ed. Saul Schwartz, 13–41. London: Routledge.

Kirwan, Samuel, Morag McDermont, & John Clarke 2016. Imagining and Practising Citizenship in Austere Times: The Work of Citizens Advice. *Citizenship Studies* 20(6–7): 764–778.

Koch, Insa. 2015. "The State Has Replaced the Man": Women, Family Homes, and the Benefit System on a Council Estate in England. *Focaal* 73: 84–96.

Koch, Insa, & Deborah James. 2022. The State of the Welfare State: Advice, Governance and Care in Settings of Austerity. *Ethnos* 87(7): 1–21.

Krige, Detlev. 2011. Power, Identity and Agency at Work in the Popular Economies of Soweto and Black Johannesburg. PhD dissertation, University of the Witwatersrand, Johannesburg. http://wiredspace.wits.ac.za/handle/10539/10143.

———. 2014. Letting Money Work for Us: Self-Organization and Financialization from Below in an All-Male Savings Club in Soweto. In *People, Money and Power in the Economic Crisis*, eds. Keith Hart & John Sharp, 61–81. New York: Berghahn Books.

Krippner, Greta R. 2005. The Financialization of the American Economy. *Socio-Economic Review* 3: 173–208.

———. 2017. Democracy of Credit: Ownership and the Politics of Credit Access in Late Twentieth-Century America. *American Journal of Sociology* 123(1): 1–47.

Kuper, Hilda, & Selma Kaplan. 1944. Voluntary Associations in an Urban Township. *African Studies* 3(4): 178–186.

Lane, J., B. McCay, & M. Thorne. 2018. Hidden Debts: The Growing Problem of Being Behind on Bills and in Debt to the Government. *Citizens Advice*. https://www.citizensadvice.org.uk/Global/CitizensAdvice/Debt%20and%20Money%20Publications/Hidden%20Debts%20report.pdf (accessed November 3, 2023).

Langley, Paul. 2009. Debt, Discipline and Government: Foreclosure and Forbearance in the Subprime Mortgage Crisis. *Environment and Planning A* 41(6): 1404–1419.

Lapavitsas, Costas. 2013. The Financialization of Capitalism: "Profiting Without Producing." *City* 17(6): 792–805.

Lavinas, Lena. 2018. The Collateralization of Social Policy Under Financialized Capitalism. *Development and Change* 49(2): 502–517.

Lawson, Victoria. 2007. Geographies of Care and Responsibility. *Annals of the Association of American Geographers* 97: 1–11.

Lazarus, Jeanne. 2020. Financial Literacy Education: A Questionable Answer to the Financialization of Everyday Life. In *The Routledge International Handbook of Financialization*. London: Routledge.

Lazzarato, Maurizio. 2012. *The Making of the Indebted Man: An Essay on the Neoliberal Condition*. Semiotext(e).

Leach, Edmund. 1957. The Epistemological Background to Malinowski's Empiricism. In *Man and Culture. An Evaluation of the Work of Bronislaw Malinowski*, ed. Raymond Firth, 119–137. London: Routledge & Kegan Paul.

Long, Norman. 2001. *Development Sociology: Actor Perspectives*. London: Routledge.

Luong, Ngoc, & Minh Nguyen. 2024. Labour Law, the Commodification of Labour and Welfare in Market Socialist Vietnam: Debates on Overtime Work in the Revised Labour Code. *Global Social Policy* 24(2): 185–202.

Mager, Anne Kelk, & Maanda Mulaudzi. 2012. Popular Responses to Apartheid: 1948–c. 1975. In *The Cambridge History of South Africa*, eds. Robert Ross, Anne Kelk Mager, & Bill Nasson, 369–408. Cambridge, UK: Cambridge University Press.

Malinowski, Bronislaw. 1922. *Argonauts of the Western Pacific. An Account of Native Enterprise and Adventure in the Archipelagoes of Melanesian New Guinea*. London: Routledge & Kegan Paul.

Marks, Susan. forthcoming. *Trucanini's Stare: Reconsidering Dignity in Theory and Practice*. Cambridge, UK: Cambridge University Press.

Martin, Randy. 2002. *Financialization of Daily Life*. Philadelphia: Temple University Press.

Mann, Geoff. 2022. Reversing the Freight Train: The Case for Degrowth. *London Review of Books* 44(16).

Mauss, Marcel. 2016 [1925]. *The Gift*, expanded ed., trans. Jane Guyer. Chicago: Hau Books.

Menahem, Georges. 2007. The Decommodified Security Ratio: A Tool for Assessing Social Protection Systems. *International Social Security Review* 60(4): 69–103.

McDermont, Morag. 2013. Acts of Translation: UK Advice Agencies and the Creation of Matters-of-Public-Concern. *Critical Social Policy* 33(2): 218–242.

Millar, Jane, & Peter Whiteford. 2020. Timing It Right or Timing It Wrong: How Should Income-Tested Benefits Deal with Changes in Circumstances? *Journal of Poverty and Social Justice* 28(1): 3–20.

Montgomerie, Johnna. 2016. Austerity and the Household: The Politics of Economic Storytelling. *British Politics* 11(4): 418–437.

Moorhead, Richard. 2001. Third Way Regulation? Community Legal Service Partnerships. *Modern Law Review* 64(4): 543–562.

———. 2004. Legal Aid and the Decline of Private Practice: Blue Murder or Toxic Job? *International Journal of the Legal Profession* 11(3): 159–187.

Moorhead, Richard, & Margaret Robinson. 2006. A Trouble Shared: Legal Problems Clusters in Solicitors' and Advice Agencies. *Department of Constitutional Affairs* Series 8/06.

Muehlebach, Andrea. 2023. *A Vital Frontier: Water Insurgencies in Europe.* Durham: Duke University Press.

Narotzky, Susannah, ed. 2020. *Grassroots Economies: Living with Austerity in Southern Europe.* London: Pluto Press.

Nattrass, N., & Seekings, J. 2014. Job Destruction in Newcastle: Minimum Wage Setting and Low-Wage Employment in the South African Clothing Industry. *Transformation* 84: 1–30.

Ndumo, Phumelelo. 2011. *From Debt to Riches: Steps to Financial Success.* Johannesburg: Jacana.

Neves, David. 2018. The Financialisation of the Poor and the Reproduction of Inequality. In *New South Africa Review 6: The Crisis of Inequality,* eds. Gilbert M. Khadiagala, Sarah Mosoetsa, Devan Pillay, & Roger Southall, 84–100. Johannesburg: Wits University Press.

Neves, David, Michael Samson, Ingrid van Niekerk, Sandile Hlatshwayo, & Andries du Toit. 2009. *The Use and Effectiveness of Social Grants in South Africa.* Cape Town: PLAAS; EPRI; Finmark Trust.

Nguyen, Minh T. N. 2020. Portfolios of Social Protection, Labour Mobility and the Rise of Life Insurance in Rural Central Vietnam. *Development & Change* 52(2): 316–339.

Nilsen, Alf Gunwald. 2020. Give James Ferguson a Fish. *Development and Change* 52(1): 3–25.

Olivier de Sardan, Jean-Pierre. 2015. Practical Norms: Informal Regulations Within Public Bureaucracies (in Africa and Beyond). In *Real Governance and Practical Norms in Sub-Saharan Africa: The Game of the Rules,* eds. Tom de Herdt & Jean-Pierre Olivier de Sardan, 19–62. London: Routledge.

Olivier de Sardan, Jean-Pierre, & Emmanuelle Piccoli. 2018. Cash Transfers and the Revenge of Contexts: An Introduction. In *Cash Transfers in Context: An Anthropological Perspective,* ed. Jean-Pierre Olivier de Sardan & Emmanuelle Piccoli, 29–91. New York: Berghahn Books.

Parry, Jonathan. 2018. Introduction: Precarity, Class and the Neoliberal Subject. In *Industrial Labor on the Margins of Capitalism,* eds. Chris Hann & Jonathan Parry, 1–38. New York: Berghahn Books.

Patrick, Ruth. 2017. *For Whose Benefit? The Everyday Realities of Welfare Reform.* Bristol: Policy Press.

Philipsen, Dirk. 2021. The Tragedy of the Private: Theft, Property, and the Loss of a Commons. *Cultural Dynamics* 33(3): 163–173.

Phillips, Ray E. 1938. *The Bantu in the City: A Study of Cultural Adjustment on the Witwatersrand.* Alice, South Africa: Lovedale Press.

Pleasence, Pascoe, Alexy Buck, Nigel Balmer, Aoife O'Grady, Hazel Genn, & Marisol Smith. 2004. *The Causes of Action: Civil Law and Social Justice.* London: Legal Services Commission.

Polanyi, Karl. 1944. *The Great Transformation: The Political and Economic Origins of Our Time.* Boston: Beacon Press.

Pollitt, Christopher, Xavier Girre, Jeremy Lonsdale, Robert Mul, Hilkka Summa, & Marit Waerness. 1999. *Performance or Compliance? Performance Audit and Public Management in Five Countries.* Oxford: Oxford University Press.

Power, Michael. 1999. *The Audit Society: Rituals of Verification.* Oxford: Oxford University Press.

Powers, Theodore, & Theodoros Rakopoulos. 2019. The Anthropology of Austerity: An Introduction. *Focaal—Journal of Global and Historical Anthropology* 83: 1–12.

Rodima-Taylor, Daivi. 2014. Passageways of Cooperation: Mutuality in Post-Socialist Tanzania. *Africa: Journal of the International African Institute* 84(4): 553–575.

Ross, Fiona. 2010. *Raw Life, New Hope.* Cape Town: UCT Press.

Roth, James. 2004. Spoilt for Choice: Financial Services in an African Township. PhD dissertation, University of Cambridge.

Sahlins, Marshall. 1976. *Culture and Practical Reason.* Chicago: University of Chicago Press.

Saiag, Hadrien. 2020. Financialization from the Margins: Notes on the Incorporation of Argentina's Subproletariat into Consumer Credit (2009–2015). *Focaal* (87): 16–32.

Sanchez, Andrew, & Sian Lazar. 2019. Understanding Labour Politics in an Age of Precarity. *Dialectical Anthropology* 43: 3–14.

Sandmo, Agnar. 2015. The Principal Problem in Political Economy: Income Distribution in the History of Economic Thought. *Handbook of Income Distribution* 2(a): 3–65.

Schraten, Jürgen. 2014. The Transformation of the South African Credit Market. *Transformation* 85: 1–20.

Schuster, Caroline, & Sohini Kar. 2021. Subprime Empire: On the In-Betweenness of Finance. *Current Anthropology* 62(4): 389–411.

Schwartz, Saul, & Joseph Spooner. 2021. Introduction. In *Oppressed by Debt: Government and the Justice System as a Creditor of the Poor,* ed. Saul Schwartz, 1–12. London: Routledge.

Seekings, Jeremy. 2020. The National Party and the Ideology of Welfare in South Africa Under Apartheid. *Journal of Southern African Studies* 46(6): 1145–1162.

Seekings, Jeremy, & Nicoli Nattrass. 2005. *Class, Race, and Inequality in South Africa.* New Haven: Yale University Press.

Shipton, Parker. 2007. *The Nature of Entrustment: Intimacy, Exchange and the Sacred in Africa.* New Haven: Yale University Press.

Siyongwana, Paqama Q. 2004. Informal Moneylenders in the Limpopo, Gauteng and Eastern Cape Provinces of South Africa. *Development Southern Africa* 21(5): 861–866.

Soederberg, Susanne. 2014. *Debtfare States and the Poverty Industry: Money, Discipline, and the Surplus Population.* London: Routledge.

Sopranzetti, Claudio. 2016. Austerity and the Scales of Sovereignty in Contemporary Italy. Paper presented at Alternatives to Austerity workshop, LSE, June 9, 2016.

Spooner, Joseph. 2021. The Local Austere Creditor. In *Oppressed by Debt: Government and the Justice System as a Creditor of the Poor,* ed. Saul Schwartz, 42–68. London: Routledge.

Stellenbosch University Law Clinic. 2021. *Debt, Credit and Consumer Rights.* Cape Town: Black Sash. https://www.blacksash.org.za/images/0511_Black_Sash_Manual_-_Debt_and_Credit_LR.pdf

Strathern, Marilyn. 1996. Cutting the Network. *Journal of the Royal Anthropological Institute* 2(3): 517–535.

———. 2000. *Audit Cultures: Anthropological Studies in Accountability, Ethics and the Academy.* London: Routledge.

Therborn, Göran. 2012. The Killing Fields of Inequality. *International Journal of Health Services* 42: 579–589.

Thomson, Robert J., and Deborah Posel. 2002. The Management of Risk by Burial Societies in South Africa. *South African Actuarial Journal* 2(1): 83–127.

Torkelson, Erin. 2018. Life on an Instalment Plan: Social Grants, Debt and South Africa. *Proceedings of the African Futures Conference.* https://anthrosource.online library.wiley.com/doi/pdf/10.1002/j.2573-508X.2018.tb000065.x (accessed January 7, 2024).

———. 2020. Collateral Damages: Cash Transfer and Debt Transfer in South Africa. *World Development* 126. https://doi.org/10.1016/j.worlddev.2019.104711 (accessed July 1, 2024).

———. 2021. Sophia's Choice: Debt, Social Welfare, and Racial Finance Capitalism. *Environment and Planning* 39(1).

Vally, Natasha. 2016. South African Social Assistance and the 2012 Privatised National Payment System; An Examination of Insecurities and Technopolitics in Social Administration and Payment. PhD dissertation, University of the Witwatersrand, Johannesburg.

van der Merwe, Stephan. 2021. Developing a Procedural Framework for Advanced Debtor Protection: The Case of Emolument Attachment Orders. Doctor of Laws dissertation, Stellenbosch University.

van der Zwan, Natascha. 2014. Making Sense of Financialization. *Socio-Economic Review* 12(1): 99–129. doi:10.1093/ser/mwt020 (accessed November 12th, 2024).

von Schnitzler, Antina. 2013. Traveling Technologies: Infrastructure, Ethical Regimes, and the Materiality of Politics in South Africa. *Cultural Anthropology* 28: 670–693.

———. 2016. *Democracy's Infrastructure: Techno-Politics and Protest After Apartheid.* Princeton: Princeton University Press.

Webb, Christopher, & Nandi Vanqa Mgijima. 2024. Financial Inclusion and the Contested Infrastructures of Cash Transfer Payments in South Africa. *Global Social Policy.* https://doi.org/10.1177/14680181241246771 (accessed July 1, 2024).

Wilkis, Ariel. 2017. *The Moral Power of Money: Morality and Economy in the Life of the Poor*. Stanford: Stanford University Press.

Wolpe, Harold. 1972. Capitalism and Cheap Labour Power in South Africa: From Segregation to Apartheid. *Economy and Society* 1(4): 425–456.

Wyman, Peter. 2018. Independent Review of the Funding of Debt Advice in England, Wales, Scotland and Northern Ireland. https://www.moneyadviceplus.org.uk/wp-content/uploads/2018/02/Peter_Wyman_Review_of_Debt_Advice_Funding_2018.pdf (accessed July 1, 2024).

Zaloom, Caitlin. 2017. Finance. *Fieldsights* (August 7). https://culanth.org/fieldsights/1163-finance (accessed July 1, 2024).

———. 2019. *Indebted: How Families Make College Work at Any Cost*. Princeton: Princeton University Press.

Zaloom, Caitlin, & Deborah James. 2023. Financialization and the Household. *Annual Review of Anthropology* 52: 399–415. https://www.annualreviews.org/content/journals/10.1146/annurev-anthro-052721-100947 (accessed November 12th, 2024).

Zelizer Viviane. 2012. How I Became a Relational Economic Sociologist and What Does That Mean? *Politics & Society* 40(2): 145–174.

Index

ADRA. *See* Association of Debt Recovery Agents

advice (SA), 13, 39, 64, 143. *See also* debt advice (SA)

advice (UK), 13, 21, 140, 143; austerity measures impacting, 98, 110, 114, 156n4; autonomy from, 111; CLACs and CLANs for, 101; frontloading of, 112–14; generalist, 100–106; by intermediaries, 96; local authorities funding, 113; NGO, 102; women seeking, 31. *See also* benefits advice; debt advice (UK)

advice organizations (UK): advice frontloading of, 112–14; audits of, 101; commissions and contracts for, 103–6; patchwork funding of, 97–98; patchwork partnerships of, 103–4, 105, 106; referrals of, 111–12

advisers (SA), 64–67, 142, 154n7

advisers (UK), 19, 23–24, 98, 142; boundary work of, 99–100; on overpaid benefits, 46–47, 124, 125, 129, 132, 133, 134, 137; patchwork funding gathered by, 21, 97; relational work of, 22, 137

affidavits: in EAO case, 76, 78, 79, 80, 81, 82, 83, 94; of Flemix-Jordaan, 78, 82; of Jonker, 83; from Maravedi Credit Solutions, 81

African National Congress (ANC), 17–18

agency, 11–15; financialization and, 25; of householders, 12

agents, 19, 146

agents (SA): Black Sash bringing together, 65; visible and invisible, 79–82

ANC. *See* African National Congress

anthropology, economic, 2, 11–12, 13–14, 15

apartheid, 18, 54, 90, 120

Appelbaum, Wendy, 73

Argonauts of the Western Pacific (Malinowski), 11, 60

Association of Debt Recovery Agents (ADRA) (SA), 78, 82, 83

austerity, households impacted by, 117–18

austerity measures (UK), 17, 20, 151n2; advice impacted by, 98, 110, 114, 156n4; advice organizations impacted by, 112–13; local authorities impacted by, 121; welfare impacted by, 18–19, 33, 34, 44, 47, 139; women impacted by, 34

CULTURE AND ECONOMIC LIFE

———————

*Black Culture, Inc.: How Ethnic Community
Support Pays for Corporate America*
Patricia A. Banks
2022

The Sympathetic Consumer: Moral Critique in Capitalist Culture
Tad Skotnicki
2021

Reimagining Money: Kenya in the Digital Finance Revolution
Sibel Kusimba
2021

*Black Privilege: Modern Middle-Class Blacks
with Credentials and Cash to Spend*
Cassi Pittman Claytor
2020

Global Borderlands: Fantasy, Violence, and Empire in Subic Bay, Philippines
Victoria Reyes
2019

*The Costs of Connection: How Data is Colonizing Human
Life and Appropriating It for Capitalism*
Nick Couldry and Ulises A. Mejias
2019

The Moral Power of Money: Morality and Economy in the Life of the Poor
Ariel Wilkis
2018

The Work of Art: Value in Creative Careers
Alison Gerber
2017

*For a complete listing of titles in this series, visit the
Stanford University Press website, www.sup.org.*

The authorized representative in the EU for product safety and compliance is:
Mare Nostrum Group B.V.
Mauritskade 21D
1091 GC Amsterdam
The Netherlands
Email address: gpsr@mare-nostrum.co.uk

KVK chamber of commerce number: 96249943

The authorized representative in the EU for product safety and compliance is:
Mare Nostrum Group
B.V Doelen 72
4831 GR Breda
The Netherlands

www.ingramcontent.com/pod-product-compliance
Lightning Source LLC
Chambersburg PA
CBHW030833270326
41928CB00007B/1023